Putting the Fire of ADDICTION

A HOLISTIC GUIDE TO RECOVERY

Barry A. Sultanoff, M.D.

Roger F. Klinger, M.T.S.

Foreword by Douglas M. Conlan

KEATS PUBLISHING

LOS ANGELES

NTC/Contemporary Publishing Group

Library of Congress Cataloging-in-Publication Data

Sultanoff, Barry A.
    Putting out the fire of addiction : a holistic guide to recovery / Barry A. Sultanoff,
Roger F. Klinger ; foreword by Douglas M. Conlan.
      p.   cm.
    Includes bibliographical references and index.
    ISBN 0-658-00281-3 (alk. paper)
    1. Substance abuse—Alternative treatment—Popular works.   2. Holistic
medicine—Popular works.   3. Alternative medicine—Popular works.   4. Compulsive
behavior—Treatment—Popular works.   I. Klinger, Roger F.   II. Title
    RC564.29 .S85   2000
    616.86'06—dc21

                                               00-030375
                                                 CIP

Managing Director and Publisher: Jack Artenstein
Executive Editor: Peter L. Hoffman
Director of Publishing Services: Rena Copperman
Managing Editor: Jama Carter
Project Editor: Claudia McCowan
Interior design by Susan H. Hartman

Published by Keats Publishing.
A division of NTC/Contemporary Publishing Group, Inc.
4255 West Touhy Avenue, Lincolnwood, Illinois 60646-1975 U.S.A.
Printed in the United States of America
International Standard Book Number: 0-658-00281-3
00 01 02 03 04 05 VP 18 17 16 15 14 13 12 11 10 9 8 7 6 5 4 3 2 1

Putting Out the Fire of ADDICTION

Contents

A Note on Addiction *vii*

Acknowledgments *ix*

Foreword *xi*

Introduction *1*

1 Our Stories *7*

2 Spirituality in Recovery *21*

3 Healing Power of Community in Recovery *29*

4 Tools for Staying Steady in an Unsteady World *47*

5 Prayer and Meditation in Recovery *55*

6 Sacred Storytelling in Recovery *89*

7 Healing Rituals for Recovery *115*

8 Honoring Beauty—Cultivating the Sacred in Everyday Life *135*

9 A Healthy Immune System in Recovery *147*

10 Dreamwork *165*

11 Tools for Transformation and Self-Reflection *179*

12 Conclusion *203*

Resources for Recovery *209*

Bibliography *223*

Index *227*

About the Authors *233*

A Note on Addiction

Addiction typically manifests as a compulsive, slavish adherence to ways of thinking, feeling, and behaving that impede, rather than facilitate, life's journey of awakening.

In *Putting Out the Fire of Addiction*, we've directed our commentary mostly toward substance addiction; in particular, addiction to alcohol. We want to emphasize, however, that the perspectives and strategies we're suggesting are generally applicable to a wide variety of addictions, including addiction to nicotine, cocaine, and other narcotics; to "tranquilizing" drugs, such as benzodiazepines (Xanax, Librium, Valium, and the like), whether or not they are prescribed by a physician; and to compulsive overeating of foods, such as carbohydrates and fats.

We believe that virtually everyone in modern society is addicted to something. These myriad addictions may include, for example, addiction to media stimulation (via television, radio, the Internet, etc.); to relationships and sex; to gambling; and/or to ways of thinking that are dysfunctional and destructive—that is, to so-called limiting patterns of thought.

As paradoxical as this may seem, many individuals become addicted to stress itself—as well as to negative emotional states, such as chronic depression, anxiety, or worry. Some become workaholics, pathologically driven toward work for its own sake. These limiting ways of thinking, perceiving, and feeling often derive from deeply entrenched beliefs about oneself, such as "I'm no good, not good enough, a failure," or about the world, for example, "The world is a dangerous place. People are out to get me. I am a victim of life. Nothing will ever work out for me."

We believe that addictions such as these, which involve no identifiable substance, are every bit as significant and real as those involving a substance. In fact, these existential addictions, these chronic patterns of being locked into dysfunctional, limiting ways of thinking and being, can be even more insidious and destructive than those in which substances are involved.

In writing this volume, therefore, we've taken a very broad, inclusive view of addiction. The book aims to be a source of information and inspiration that will be of genuine relevance to all who are addicted, whether to substances or not. Throughout these pages are perspectives and techniques that can be used effectively as strategies for recovery from addictions of all kinds—including, but not limited to, substance abuse.

We strongly urge readers to embrace this very inclusive definition of addiction that we're proposing. In that way, you can best maintain a creative openness to discovering how the particular interventions we suggest can be applied in your own life and in the lives of others whom you may be seeking to assist.

Acknowledgments

This book could only have been written with the loving support of our community. We extend a special thanks to Peggy Meiklejohn for her valuable insights and tireless review of the manuscript, to Emily Woo for her steady support throughout the book's birthing process, to Pat McCallum for her devoted and powerful assistance in "making it so," to Dr. Kriss Haig for his generous support and valuable feedback throughout the writing process, to Dorothy Downes for her experienced editing of "Our Stories," to Tom Hoge for his wise mentoring, and to Jody Parsons for being our West Coast "custodian" of the manuscript.

To our families of origin, our parents, brothers, and sisters, we give thanks for the gift of life and for the opportunity to have grown up in a safe, ultimately "ideal" learning environment from which we could emerge into responsible adulthood. We especially thank our parents for supporting us in the pursuit of the formal education as health professionals that became the foundation for the more innovative, pioneering work that has followed.

To our revered spiritual teachers—Thich Nhat Hanh, His Holiness the Dalai Lama, and others too numerous to mention individually—we feel profound gratitude and a joyful sense of "spiritual collegiality."

With humility, we wish to thank the myriad "extraordinary ordinary" teachers who have turned up along the way, who have appeared at every turn in the road just when we needed them, to tap us on the shoulder and awaken us to what we needed to see next.

We wish, too, to express our deep gratitude to the fellowship of Alcoholics Anonymous for providing us—and the countless millions of others whose lives have been powerfully changed for the better—the gateway to co-creating a rich and sober life.

And with a deep sense of awe, we thank the Creator of this profound mystery of which we are all a part. Life is good! We feel grateful—and ecstatic!—for this precious opportunity to be living, loving, and evolving in the best ways we know, in community with all beings.

Foreword

His Holiness the Dalai Lama says that our common spiritual task is "not the building of beautiful churches and temples, but the cultivation of positive human qualities such as tolerance, generosity, and love." In 1993, just after the Centenary of the Parliament of the World's Religions in Chicago, I met one of the authors of *Putting Out the Fire of Addiction* at a session on meditation. In this man I experienced a spiritual energy and qualities of kindness, gentleness, humility, and compassion that reminded me of the Dalai Lama's words. I am pleased, therefore, to have been asked to write this foreword to a work that, from the outset, seeks to serve and aid our fellow beings.

This is a timely and profoundly spiritual book. It is one that dives deeply into the authors' personal experiences of addiction as a way of introducing their readers to the healing potential within the stories and the lives of their patients and counselees.

This is a book about the lived experience of ordinary men and women. It explores their continuing stories of breaking free from their addictions as they find their way toward the light of spiritual awakening. It speaks both of the inevitability of pain and of the possibility of healing within the pain, of a lived acceptance of human limitations and powerlessness as well as an awareness that, ultimately, success is always possible. This is a common and universal story, a shared journey, a story of hope.

Sultanoff and Klinger offer us chapters of a journey and a pilgrimage, their own and those of their spiritual companions. They bring with them "tools for staying steady in an uncertain world" such as may be found in prayer and meditation, sacred storytelling, and healing rituals and in finding ways of making our day-to-day lives sacred and beautiful again.

The authors help us to dream again and to explore new horizons on our journey to recovery. Barry Sultanoff's openness is perhaps most clearly articulated in his willingness, even as a conventionally trained medical doctor, to receive the advice of a good friend at a time when he was struggling to overcome his own addiction to cigarettes. That led him, by way of acknowledging his own depression, into the possibility of valuing and receiving the practical benefits of another field of knowledge on the human journey. In his case, it brought him to the beneficial use of the Bach Flower Remedies. In Roger Klinger's story, one discovers an intrepid willingness to keep on keeping on, despite the magnitude of the challenges he faced. Even in the most dire circumstances, he demonstrated a determined openness to learning new ways and doing whatever it takes to break free of the downward spiral of his addiction.

The authors show us the way to recognize a wholeness and unity in life, which is there for the exploration. Beyond the fear of failure or departing from the "norm," life offers us all a chance to start again and to grow into new life. Sultanoff and Klinger do not run from facing the vicissitudes of the journey or from the agonies of falling down and getting up again. Neither do they deny the painful reality that even for a pilgrim of the spirit, one's identity, if found, is best approached in humility.

This is a clear book to which we may return again and again, well set out and with a clear emphasis on kindness, understanding, and love. There is tolerance and graciousness here, such as we find when we're reminded that "prayer and meditation are avenues through which an individual can directly access his 'sanity' by contacting a power that is himself, yet is greater than himself. . . . What really matters is not the name but the recovering addict's recognition that there is a power greater than himself."

The authors are gracious, too, when they remind us that our symbols for ultimate meaning can only point to a reality that we can never directly grasp. Throughout the book, they gently nudge us to take the broadest possible view of what Spirit may be.

The personal nature of the stories that run like a sutra throughout the book show us something of the travails of our teachers—the authors and those whose lives they share—and their sources of strength. We find here timely guides as to how we can live with, care for, and attend to a more healthy lifestyle, a not insignificant task for people who live increasingly amid the challenges of an often chaotic and distracted modern world. The authors remind us not only of how we can eat better and otherwise keep healthy but, more significantly, of how we think and dream.

Throughout the book, Sultanoff and Klinger continually remind us that abstract theory is not an end in itself: It must shape our living in the here and now. They offer us a golden opportunity to re-vision what we hold most dear in our lives and to reawaken to this truth: The most important wisdom is that of discovering, through our own realization of the light, how we might best serve and aid our fellow beings.

Douglas M. Conlan
Bede Griffiths International Literary Trust
University of South Australia
Adelaide, Australia

Introduction

The inspiration for this book came during a walk across a snowy meadow in the beautiful Shenandoah Valley. Roger's sermon had been canceled that day because of the weather, so the two of us decided to go for a long, leisurely walk in the fresh snow.

As we were soaking up the pristine beauty of Rappahannock County, Virginia, where Roger has made his home for nearly a decade and which Barry has enjoyed over the years as a treasured getaway from the hustle-bustle of suburban living, the idea for this book just happened. It came to us right after Jackson and Maddie, the neighbor's golden retrievers, had added their unrestrained playfulness to our winter meander. As we watched those carefree canines cavorting in the snow, the book playfully announced itself to us. And we felt inspired and engaged by what we heard.

The day was absolutely breathtaking in its beauty as we walked toward the mountains that make up Skyline Drive in Shenandoah National Park. New footsteps in virgin snow,

Canadian geese honking on the lake, a young deer flushed from the brambles—these were nature's gifts that day to two grateful men, two men who had long been good friends and colleagues, kindred spirits celebrating the gifts of friendship and life.

The idea for this book seemed to greet our consciousness that day like a clear, flowing river splashing over rocks. That energetic river of clear intention soon smoothed our furrowed brows, eroding any resistance we might have had to writing it.

Our entire walk from that moment on reflected the surge of pulsing energy that we now felt moving through us. As we continued to amble across that magnificent snowscape, we shared ideas, visions of what we thought the book should include, and our personal stories of addiction and recovery.

That vibrant conversation created a flurry of lively enthusiasm that fueled us at every step of the book's unfolding. It remained an ongoing dialogue between us as the book was being written.

On that day of the book's conception, we realized that our book could serve as a vehicle for deep healing and personal transformation. Perhaps we might touch a few lives deeply. What if our book could make a difference in the life of at least one human being suffering from addiction—a man or a woman whose very existence might be hanging by a thread, a person who might be on the cusp of shifting from a state of disease and decline into a new way of life?

We hoped that in some way we might support that individual in living a lifestyle of richness, holiness, and radical aliveness, rather than falling off the wagon and into the abyss. We knew on that day that we must say "Yes!" to this inner directive that we took to be our calling. We must write this book!

This is a book about change—specifically, about changing destructive habits into life-affirming behaviors. Most important of all, it is a book about changing *one's entire perspective on life.*

Successfully overcoming addiction ultimately rests upon a revitalized way of thinking. One can live at the effect of life, as its victim; or one can learn to be the creator of that life experience, the author of his or her own life story.

When one is addicted—for example, to nicotine or to alcohol—that substance becomes a tyrannical ruler. Personal choice is usurped by the persistent, irrational urgings of something outside oneself that demands obeisance, and which often exacts a heavy price.

In this sense, addiction can be looked upon as a form of idolatry. In this theology of addiction, the false god is the addictive substance and all the paraphernalia and baggage associated with it. The duped parishioner is the addicted individual, who comes to the Church of Bondage to worship at the Altar of Transient Pleasure.

Lived consciously, on a path with heart, life can be a journey of profound fulfillment. Lived unconsciously, it can be a rocky road that includes intense suffering.

Recovery involves recognizing this truth: One can consciously embark upon an authentic sacred pilgrimage or healing journey, and thereby venture into a whole new way of being.

The brilliant psychiatrist Dr. Carl Jung stated that alcoholism/addiction is an unconscious quest for God, or wholeness of being, which the addict seeks through chemical means. Our own healing journeys, which have included our personal experiences of recovery from addictions to alcohol, marijuana, and nicotine, as well as our professional experience in guiding hundreds of clients on their journeys, have taught us that there is no wrong way to proceed in life, except perhaps to try to refuse the journey entirely.

On the other hand, there are many, many different ways of journeying. Some seem to support freedom and well-being, while others tend to promote entrapment and powerlessness.

Human beings seem, on the whole, to be very prone to chemical addictions and addictive behaviors. Why is this so?

As health professionals, we often see the personal havoc that addictions can wreak, the unfolding of disease on all levels, the destruction of self, family, community, and society. We have seen the chemical undoing of presumably intelligent human beings, the disability and the enslavement, the erosion of judgment and responsibility, the onslaught of dysfunction, illness, and death.

We have also been inspired, blessed, and honored to participate with individuals on their miraculous journeys of recovery.

We have sought to understand the nature of chemical addiction and, in practical ways, to support ourselves and others in breaking free of it. This book is a synthesis of the best of what we have learned, a guidebook of tools and resources for walking the path of successful recovery.

This guidebook is not intended as a "cookbook" or as a panacea. Readers will have to weave their own unique tapestry from the "strips of cloth" that are offered here. Neither is it a substitute for medical treatment centers, Alcoholics Anonymous, twelve-step groups, and the like. Rather, it provides accessible, practical tools for living a sober, abundant life in recovery.

We do not pretend that breaking free of addiction is easy. The reality is that most addicts never make it through the portal into recovery. However, millions of people worldwide, through the assistance of AA, the Twelve Steps, and similar groups, have successfully embarked on this healing journey of recovery. Recovery is possible, and this book can provide effective tools and resources for helping individuals along whatever pathways they may choose to reach that destination.

What we are proposing here is, in some ways, radical. Our goal is nothing less than breaking free from a prison of the mind—

a prisoner's cell of dysfunctional thinking and behavior—out into the open field of awakening consciousness.

As the mystic poet Rumi put it seven centuries ago:

> *Out beyond ideas of right or wrong,*
> *there is a field . . .*
> *I'll meet you there;*
> *and together*
> *we'll let the beauty we love*
> *be what we dare!*

1

Our Stories

The sharing of personal stories about the crisis of addiction is part and parcel of the recovery process. Stories are the thread that can weave the entire quilt of recovery together into a coherent fabric.

In the Chinese language, the character for crisis also means opportunity. Addiction can often be a crisis of life-threatening proportions. The same crisis that can break a person down in a destructive manner can also present a golden opportunity for healing. Such a crisis can be a doorway into a new way of living and being.

Not surprisingly, AA and other twelve-step programs emphasize the healing potential of "shared experience, strength and hope." At Twelve Steps meetings, personal storytelling is used to convey to newcomers what others before them have been through—what their addictions were like, how they found their way to recovery, and where they are on their life journeys. This personal sharing encourages the newcomers to tell their own stories.

The following stories of healing and transformation are drawn from the authors' personal experiences with drug and alcohol addiction and recovery. We offer our own stories in hopes that readers will find in them a source of inspiration and a more intimate connection with issues that individuals in recovery characteristically deal with.

We have decided to simply tell it like it is. We've presented our stories as honestly as we know how, offering our truth as we have lived it, and asking that the stories speak for themselves.

Barry's Story

My involvement with cigarettes and nicotine addiction began when I was barely a teenager. Because I was intellectually precocious, my parents enrolled me in a high-powered boys' school whose strong suit was educating future scientists and engineers. By the age of thirteen, I was already commuting sixty miles by train, five days a week, to Baltimore Polytechnic Institute in Baltimore, Maryland.

My daily grind began at about 6:30 A.M., when I left my parents' suburban home and headed for the train station. I returned home twelve hours later, after a day of intense academic focus and riding the rails—a considerable stretch for a boy of thirteen.

After school, at the train station, and also during the long unsupervised train ride, there were lots of opportunities for getting into (relatively innocent) trouble of all kinds. My friends and I spent countless hours playing endless free pinball games after rigging the machines at the train station.

For the majority of my day, I was resoundingly free to do whatever I wanted without my parents, or any other authority figures, bugging me. I was hardly out of my parents' sight before I began smoking cigarettes like my friends. It seemed like the cool thing to do. One friend had been smoking since he was ten or eleven years old. Before long, my own addiction to nicotine was well established. And it was reinforced by the company I kept with my smoking comrades.

By the time I was fourteen or fifteen, I had become a nicotine addict. I had sold my birthright of clean, breathable air to the polluting "devil" of smoking.

This smoking habit adopted in my early teens persisted for the next sixteen years through high school, college, and medical school. It gained momentum like a steel engine propelled without regard for safety, speed, or consequences. In those years, I never paused long enough to consider the consequences of my lighting and relighting—my compulsive and destructive ritual. The effects became multiplied and compounded over those years, impairing not only my physical health and stamina but also my ability to concentrate on what was right in front of me.

In fact, as I look back on it now, I see that I had to become *unconscious* of what I was doing to my lungs—and to the rest of me—to be able to allow this self-destructive part of myself to continue its reign of denial-generated tyranny.

Clearly, the accumulation and daily dosing of carbon monoxide and other toxins was not doing me—or my ability to focus on what I needed to attend to—any favor! And yet, there was no way I could have stopped, even if I had wanted to. I was powerless over smoking. For those sixteen years, I had lost all control over both the frequency and the amount of nicotine I consumed.

I can still recall smoking alone in my dorm room at Cornell, looking down at the ashtray and seeing two lit cigarettes dangling there—and being surprised that I hadn't finished the first one!

Now, reflecting upon this as a man in his fifties, I can see that addiction reinforced my hard-driving type A behavior. I knew that somehow I had to keep myself going through those tough academic years. I had to keep pushing. So I used nicotine to chemically prop up my habitual way of bulldozing through challenges and forcing myself to perform at the level of academic excellence that I, in collusion with my parents, had demanded.

Cigarettes became, and continued to be, my immediate yet transitory reward, the treat I gave myself to palliate the rigorous self-abuse of my tender spirit, abuse that had become the price of academic success.

In those years, the fear of academic failure hung over my head like a sword of Damocles. In my family of origin, it was unthinkable not to make high grades in school. I believed that, were I to have failed academically, I would have been disowned by my family. I might have even attempted suicide. Instead, a part of me chose to do so slowly with cigarettes.

Cigarettes did serve one useful purpose: In a certain sense, they did get me through those years. Five years after graduating from medical school and achieving the high regard of my family for having successfully become a doctor, I was finally able to overcome my addiction and put out the fire for good.

By the time I became ready to break the shackles of smoke, however, my relationship with cigarettes had become long-term and deeply entrenched. My two to two-and-a-half packs of cigarettes a day had become a kind of friend in my shirt pocket, whom I could call upon for companionship anytime I felt lonely. Even then I knew, in the far recesses of my mind, that I had to make a change.

I had been floundering for a long time. I was sick and tired of this embarrassing dependence that was so inconsistent with my chosen vocation as a health professional, this dysfunctional way of coping with an overly stressful life. I knew that I had to give up smoking. But how?

As it turned out, I not only had to put out the fire by stopping smoking, I also had to pour some water on the coals by working toward overcoming my profound loneliness and despair. This emotional work was central to my recovery process. With the assistance of a sensitive and highly skilled psychotherapist, I embarked willingly on that journey of liberation.

It is said that when one is ready to cross the river, a boat appears. For me that boat came ashore in an unlikely place. It showed up as a suggestion made to me by a close friend, a biology professor at the same college in upstate New York where I was teaching courses in health education at the time.

John's recommendation was that I take a mixture of flower essences (discussed more fully in chapter 11) to help me overcome the depression and ennui in which I seemed to be languishing. I willingly agreed to try his prescription of natural medicine, so he made up a remedy for me, which contained a mixture of five of the Bach Flower Remedies, including gentian, mustard, and crab apple.

I began taking several drops of this mixture orally, four or five times a day, as he had suggested. This triggered a three-week journey of emotional release the likes of which I had never known before nor have experienced since. My depression lifted and gradually resolved as my anger rose powerfully to the surface, anger that I had presumably stuffed away inside me for nearly three decades.

The culmination of my release of anger and rage came on the day that I picked up one of my kitchen chairs and, like a man gone wild, used its legs to batter and destroy the drainpipes under my kitchen sink. Although it was costly to replace them later, my release proved to be worth the price.

That final release of pent-up rage was the harbinger of a remarkable change: My craving for cigarettes totally disappeared.

I knew that I would never again want to smoke another cigarette . . . and I never have!

In freeing myself, finally, from nicotine addiction, I reclaimed the energy that had been bound to that habit—energy that I was then able to mobilize in support of more life-sustaining activities.

My depression disappeared almost completely, and I redirected some of my newfound energy into long-distance running. I trained for and completed four marathon runs during the six years immediately following my liberation from the smoking habit.

Running those twenty-six miles was vitally empowering for me—a form of regaining the boy left behind on the tracks of my childhood. It was the fulfillment of a lifetime dream to transcend the rather narrow self-concept that I had held of myself as a kind of one-dimensional academic nerd, and to claim my new identity as a well-rounded, multidimensional, and fully mature man. By running marathons, I discovered that I was much more than the limited version of myself that my parents and I had formerly envisioned. I was fully capable of having notable successes, even in the athletic arena.

About ten years ago, because of some knee problems, I switched from running to avid bicycling. Most recently, I've taken up in-line skating. Last year I completed my first long-distance in-line skating event, a thirty-eight-mile course from Athens to Dacula (not across the Atlantic, just across part of Georgia!).

On the more sublime and personal side, I have embraced Argentine tango dancing as a genuine passion during the past few years. I have become a dance aficionado and have already published several articles on the health benefits of social dancing.

Indeed, life after cigarettes has been good!

Freeing myself from addiction to nicotine opened a gateway into the life of exuberance that I live today. There have been many angels along the way, both human and otherwise, and I celebrate that fortunate blessing. Looking back on all this, I see that the really crucial point is that I did not replace one addiction with another; rather, I unhooked myself from the *cause* of my addictive behavior.

> **I celebrate the freedom I have solidly claimed and have never relinquished, beginning with the day I said a loud "no" to cigarettes and a resounding "yes" to the smoke-free life!**

Roger's Story

I grew up in the sixties in a typical suburban family in Maryland, with loving parents and an older brother and sister. When I was eleven years old, I was schooled in the painful and destructive nature of addiction; an older sibling had developed an addiction to drugs. The next few years were a painful hell because addiction had a devastating impact on the whole family.

From what I had seen in my family, I was already terrified by the nature of addiction. At the age of eleven I vowed that I would never drink or use drugs.

I grew up socially isolated and wanted desperately to fit in. I remember vividly the first day I had a drink away from home, at the age of sixteen while on a wilderness trip out West. I got drunk, and I loved it. Soon afterwards, I tried marijuana. I felt that I had come home. I felt so whole and happy. Finally, I was part of the in crowd.

The next day I bought a quarter pound of pot. From the beginning, I used it daily because it helped me sleep, be more social, and have fun. I became what is now known clinically as an instant addict.

I realize now that I was hot-wired for addiction, since alcoholism does run in my family. I used marijuana very heavily throughout college, and I could see that I had a problem early on. I would sometimes have blackouts, and I was aware that I used drugs in far greater quantities than my peers. And yet, I could not stop. Increased tolerance, blackouts . . . these were all early warning signs of addiction.

Like many young people of that era, I joined a communal house and experimented with psychedelics, speed, and barbiturates. In our community, a whole pharmacy of illegal drugs was always readily available. I knew that drugs were interfering with my life, and I tried to stop using at the age of eighteen, going cold turkey. This catapulted me into terrible withdrawal and suicidal despair, which prompted me to enter psychotherapy. That doctor made it clear— in no uncertain terms!—that I had to stop using drugs.

And yet, we never addressed the issue of my alcohol consumption in any of our therapy sessions. I wanted to change. I wanted to grow, and yet I could not seem to stop my self-destructive behaviors through willpower alone, at least not for more than a day or so at a time. Outwardly, I appeared to be a successful, well-integrated, ambitious young man. I had a terrific teaching assistantship in psychology, I had good friends, and I was one of just a handful of students who had been offered the opportunity to develop his own interdisciplinary major in individual studies. And yet my inner life was at war with my growing addiction.

My heartfelt desire to face my inner conflicts and become whole was very strong. I was deeply committed to therapy. However, despite my best efforts, I could not quit either marijuana or alcohol completely. This led to my development of what clinicians call a control strategy: I entered into a binge pattern of chemical addiction, stopping for periods of time and then resuming my former drug usage.

Over time these extremes grew even worse. I had a devastating car accident, withdrew from college on account of the effects of drug withdrawal, and experienced multiple overdoses. Under the influence of alcohol, pot, and tranquilizers, I would often lose total control.

My tolerance had grown extremely high. I found myself needing large, increasing quantities of drugs with each binge, and I was growing more isolated from people, because my peers did not use drugs to the degree that I did.

I was soon fired from my dream job with the National Park Service. Then, on my nineteenth birthday, I tried to commit suicide using barbiturates and alcohol. My doctor gave me an ultimatum: "Stop using drugs!"

But again, even though I desperately wanted help and tried my best to stop, psychotherapy alone could not break my addiction to drugs. I was gradually wearing down and approaching what is called a bottom in addiction. I really had no tools to sustain me other than my own willpower and the psychoanalytic model, which historically has proved to be a total failure in addiction treatment.

The psychoanalytic model maintains the false premise that addiction is the result of deep, unresolved inner conflicts. Its contention is that if a person can only resolve and work through these conflicts, then he can safely drink.

It is true that I had tremendous inner conflicts, which were well established prior to my ever using chemical substances, yet the current reality was that the chemical fire of addiction had to be put out first. Then, if I could only stay sober long enough, I had a real chance of facing my situation head on and doing whatever it took to get well by working through these conflicts.

Modern medical science classifies alcoholism/addiction as "a primary, chronic and potentially fatal illness." *Primary* means that first the addiction must be addressed and treated as a disease. Then the manifestations of the illness can be addressed.

Willpower does not cure addiction. Therapy, on the other hand, can be beneficial. It can help point a person toward a twelve-step recovery process, and it can and does help facilitate healing and growth once the fire of addiction is extinguished.

There is a Buddhist story that says:

> It is impossible to whitewash a burning house. First the fire must be put out, then a foundation can be rebuilt, brick by brick, then the house can be reconstructed, and eventually it can be painted and made beautiful again.

The same holds true for addiction. For me, psychoanalysis, yoga, nutrition, running, drug counseling groups, and willpower were all noble yet flawed attempts to whitewash my burning house.

On January 4, 1981, after a horrendous binge, I called Alcoholics Anonymous. I was urged to come immediately to a noon meeting in Bethesda, Maryland.

The seeds for change and transformation were planted in the ground of my being on that day. Although I was quite toxic, I felt hopeful seeing the genuine joy and happiness present in this smoky roomful of sixty or seventy men and women already on the road to recovery.

The next nine months were very painful for me, as I continued to relapse, denying for months that I had any alcohol problem at all. Yet I found that people were patient with me. I attended meetings twice daily and pulled together as much as three months' sobriety, which for me was a miracle.

Addiction is often described in AA as "a cunning, baffling, and powerful disease." This proved true in my case. I had one more relapse that started with one single beer. That one beer turned into six, following which I added hashish to the mixture.

Within three days I was totally out of control. I left my house, walked away from a fine job at the Smithsonian Institute, and disappeared into the streets. I took to living in hotel rooms and using chemicals virtually nonstop. Much of the time I was in a blackout, checking into hotels using an alias, yet being unable to remember my name when checking out!

For three weeks, I lived in a toxic cloud. My despair grew deeper as I found myself needing more and more chemicals to maintain my numbness and to continue blotting out my feelings. In a very real sense, drugs and alcohol owned me body and soul at that time.

AA says this: "First, the man takes a drink; then the drink takes a drink; then the drink takes the man."

This adage had become a reality for me. I continued on my horrific binge until my body and psyche were just about caving in and I had exhausted all my resources. I was now staying in a dingy hotel room and experiencing increasingly frequent withdrawal symptoms because I no longer had the chemical means available to numb the pain that was emerging. I was out of money, out of Jack Daniels and pot, and beginning to face my night of hell, with terrible hallucinations and frequent thoughts of death. I was in near total despair.

I lay crumpled on the floor, yet somehow I made it through the night intact. I realized in the morning that I had only two options: commit suicide or go back to AA.

I was fortunate that I had sown my seeds of hope through all my earlier contacts with AA and mustered the courage to call one of my sponsors. I felt broken and depressed, and yet relieved that I was now choosing life over death.

Still in a toxic fog but functioning, at least on a rudimentary level, I met with my sponsors in AA and was urged to enter a twenty-eight-day rehabilitation program for addiction. Clearly, I needed more help than AA alone could offer me.

My stay at Seneca House was transformative. It was in this humble house of healing that I began to face the true nature of my addiction. I surrendered fully. I accepted the irrefutable truth that I was totally powerless over all mood-changing chemicals and that my life had become completely unmanageable.

Seneca House embodied a holistic approach to healing that integrated the best tools of modern medicine—a well-trained staff of nurses, doctors, and therapists and an emphasis on nutrition and stress reduction through yoga and meditation—all housed in a setting that offered unconditional love and support. The basic goals of this program were to provide each person with a solid beginning, a base of sobriety from which she could create a new life, free from the bondage of mood-altering chemicals.

I have never had another drink or used another drug since entering Seneca House. I have managed to maintain sobriety ever since.

I consider myself one of the lucky ones, though I do acknowledge the part that my own good choices and commitment to change has made in this positive outcome.

I have been in AA for nearly eighteen years now. My life has been restored to wholeness—physically, psychologically, and spiritually. I've been able to grow and to heal, to discover who I truly am, and to find my vocation as a pastoral psychotherapist, teacher, and writer.

I have gradually created a new life for myself, living out AA's promise of "the joy of living." I can honestly say that I am a grateful recovering alcoholic, one for whom hitting bottom opened up a new life. Picking up the pieces of a life shattered by addiction was a long, slow, often painful, and yet liberating process.

It is ironic that addiction nearly destroyed my life, and yet through acceptance of my addiction, freedom grew, and the gateway to a richly fulfilling, prosperous new life opened wide.

In recovery and sobriety, I have reclaimed my power of choice. I am blessed to have created an opportunity for a second chance, and for this I am deeply grateful. I feel indebted to my loving family, my friends, AA, and the God of my understanding for providing me the precious and sacred gift of a new life in recovery.

My life is well integrated today. My addiction does not define me; it is but one facet of my being. AA and the Twelve Steps have become fully incorporated into my life.

Sobriety has allowed me to build bridges to the greater community and to acquire the tools for loving, laughing, and living a life of radical honesty and wholehearted passion. Sobriety has allowed me to develop a deep and ever-growing spirituality and faith; to be of service to those still suffering from their addictions; and to live an abundant, richly rewarding life.

"Amazing Grace" has become my life's theme song. My addiction had generated a sense of being "lost and blind," whereas sobriety has allowed me the grace to see, to find, and to rediscover life and all that I hold to be ultimate in value.

Most important, my journey of recovery has allowed me to come home to myself and feel at home in my life, aware that I am living on a sacred planet, recognizing that sobriety and life are both precious and tentative—sacred gifts that must never be taken for granted.

2

Spirituality in Recovery

Our goal for this chapter is to offer a definition of spirituality and to discuss its importance in the recovery process. In describing our particular take on spirituality, we intend to offer a context for many of the chapters that follow.

What is spirituality? This is a subject that has been debated by scholars, mystics, religious leaders, and other serious-minded people for centuries. This debate has filled volumes of books on library shelves. It has been a topic of perennial interest, one that probes the fundamental question of a person's essential nature and relationship to the world.

The nineteenth-century sage Ramakrishna admonishes us to

Dive deep,
otherwise you cannot get to the gems
at the bottom of the ocean.
You cannot pick up the gems
if you only float on the surface.

During active addiction, we are floating on the surface of life. Once we sober up, we awaken from our sleep and the thirst for life's depth begins to grow stronger.

> **Embracing spirituality in recovery is a means of diving deep into the ocean of our life.**

Whatever spirituality is—and we acknowledge the impossibility of ever fully defining it in words—we believe that it is of paramount importance in the healing process. We have found spirituality to be a central component of recovery from addiction and of the holistic approaches that support it.

Spirituality is not religion. Among the billions of human beings on this earth, there are thousands of different religions and religious sects, each of which has its own particular ideas about God/Deity and its rules of ethical behavior. Religions have specific beliefs and dogmas that tend to be exclusive.

Spirituality is relevant to the nature of belonging itself. It is broad and deep, inclusive of all religions, even agnosticism and atheism. Spirituality is not about ideas. It is about the *experience of living*—what we like to call being radically alive. For the recovering addict, embracing this radical aliveness is an essential goal, one that can be truly life-transforming. Adopting this energized way of life is far more important, we believe, than just overcoming addictive patterns.

Spirituality offers us an expanded sense of who we are and of the roles we play in our lives. Spirituality helps us feel part of the greater whole, rather than isolated or apart from it.

Spirituality is, as Robert Hass, former poet laureate of the United States, says, one's "private relationship to the mystery of being alive." It includes what we call *trusting the sacred mystery;* that is, a willingness to make a leap of faith by abiding in both the visible and the invisible forces operating in our lives.

Perelandra, a center for nature research near Warrenton, Virginia, offers this philosophy, inscribed on a beautiful poster bearing the photograph of one of its circular gardens: *Only those who can see the invisible can do the impossible!*

Spiritual practices such as meditation, prayer, contemplation, and sacred ritual are not the exclusive domain of any one religion. They are available to all, including those who may find themselves on the journey of recovery, whether they are members of an organized religion or not.

For our purposes, we especially view spirituality as an invitation—an invitation to recognize that within each one of us is a part that is whole and beautiful, a sacred part. This aspect of oneself, this spiritual part that resides within everyone, is intrinsically whole. It transcends issues of good versus evil.

No matter who we are—no matter what our struggles, our misguided expressions, or our past mistakes may have been—there is a radiant part within each of us, an eternal part that we choose to call spirit. This aspect of ourselves is imbued with the power to heal. It is legitimately who we are, at our core essence.

This part of ourselves is just as real and important in the recovery process—we would contend, even more important!—than our personalities, our thoughts, our emotions, and our behaviors. It is this part that underlies all the rest and that is most essential for our healing. This is the place from which we may draw profound hope and inspiration, even when all else may seem to have failed us.

This part of ourselves is a beacon, continually broadcasting the news about our true nature. We are invited (by God, by this divine part of ourselves) to tune in to that broadcast, anytime, anywhere. We are benevolently goaded by this deep and magnificent part of ourselves to remember who we truly are and to *listen!*

Part of what we're proposing is that putting out the fire of addiction rests upon honoring, and at times calling upon, this "cosmic firefighter" within, this one we refer to as Spirit. This cosmic helper is always on call, ready to respond to any crisis or emergency, big or small, whatever its nature. So we might do well to ring up this "volunteer firefighter" whenever our own fires may be burning out of control.

This aspect of spirituality that compassionately offers us an invitation to remember the golden opportunity that life offers and the opportunity to choose Spirit as our lifelong dance partner—this is what we intend to emphasize.

For the individual in recovery, this remembering may be especially crucial, since it can be so seductive at times for the recovering addict to fall off the wagon into low self-esteem, self-loathing, and despair. It may prove to be essential—even life-saving—for the individual in recovery to remember and make regular contact with this inviolable goodness that resides at the core of her being.

Access to this goodness is everyone's birthright. It does not have to be earned. All that is necessary is that it be seen, recognized, and acknowledged for what it is: the truth of each person's essential nature.

When a person aligns himself with this place of wholeness, or holiness, within, he awakens to the beauty that he is, thereby enhancing self-esteem and solidifying his foothold on the road to recovery.

Ultimately, the choice comes down to this: One may either acknowledge her divine nature and willingly celebrate it, or she may deny her intrinsic spirituality until (most typically) she is brought to some kind of awakening kicking and screaming (for example, by a life-threatening illness or other personal crisis).

Consider the following report involving relationship addiction. Crisis in a primary relationship became the vehicle through which an epiphany occurred. Here, a woman trying to find her way through a traumatic divorce discovered an aspect of herself—namely, her own breath—to be a representation and living embodiment of the divine.

> Several years ago, I went on a personal vision quest, because I wanted to prepare myself for an upcoming divorce trial that I knew would be difficult. My old bullheaded way of life was failing me, so I took a week of solitude, rising in the early morning to welcome the sun, canoeing the vast waters of the Everglades, and sharing space with contented wildlife.
>
> My life had been coming apart at the seams. At that time I was threatened with losing custody of my children, possibly forfeiting my savings, my house, even my livelihood as a doctor, along with my marriage of twenty-one years.
>
> The "me" I had known was dissolving. I needed a more solid self-image to get me through the difficult times ahead. Who was I now, if not some conglomeration of all these relationships, places, and functions?
>
> One day, while walking a trail, something clicked, and I finally got it. I felt my legs walking, my arms swinging, and most essentially, my own persistent breath. In that moment I realized a physical presence, an essence that could not be taken from me. My breath became my anchor, my constant friend; and along with it, I've discovered a steadiness and a centeredness that has helped me get through many a difficult time since then.

This story is reminiscent, too, of an often-told anecdote regarding AA co-founder Bill Wilson's spiritual awakening. As the story goes, Bill was at a bottom in his alcohol addiction process and had to be hospitalized. At one pivotal moment, he is said to have cried out, "If there is a God, let him show himself! I am ready to do anything, anything!"

At that moment, a great white light filled the room, and Bill experienced indescribable ecstasy. He suddenly realized he was free of the bondage of his addiction, and a wonderful sense of God's presence surrounded him.

Spirituality is indeed central to the recovery process. Dr. Carl Jung, in his correspondence with Bill Wilson regarding Jung's patient Roland H., stated that "his craving for alcohol was the equivalent, on a low level, of the spiritual thirst for wholeness, expressed in medieval language: the union with God." Jung saw alcoholism as an appropriate, albeit misdirected, thirst for wholeness—for genuine spiritual experience.

Jung went on to explain that "[the word] 'alcohol' in Latin is *spiritus*, . . . the same word that is used for the highest religious experience." Again, regarding his treatment of Roland H., Jung explained to Bill Wilson that in his view, only a spiritual awakening could have provided the impetus for the personal transformation required to save this patient and restore him to sobriety.

Currently, AA describes itself as a spiritual fellowship. It makes a clear distinction between spirituality and religion, eschewing any religious affiliation whatsoever. AA affirms that an individual can be deeply spiritual with or without a specific religious affiliation.

To quote Step 12 of the Twelve Steps and Twelve Traditions of AA:

> When a man or a woman has a spiritual awakening, the most important meaning of it is that he has now become able to do, feel, and believe that which he could not do before on his unaided strength and resources alone. He has been granted a gift which amounts to a new state of consciousness and being. He has been set on a path which tells him he is really going somewhere, that life is not a dead end, not something to be endured or mastered.

In a very real sense he has been transformed because he has laid hold of a strength which in one way or another he had hitherto denied himself. He finds himself in possession of a degree of honesty, tolerance, unselfishness, peace of mind and love of which he had thought himself quite incapable. What he has received is a free gift, and yet usually, at least in some small part, he has made himself ready to receive it.

We conclude with this poem by psychotherapist Elizabeth Hess. In it, she describes the quality of thirst for God that can truly lead the addict home along the road to recovery.

Dearest God,
The words have all been written
and still—I write more words.
The poets have all sung
your splendor
for ages and ages and ages—
and still—I want to sing
some more!

Two desires—and desire, more
than wanting, holy purpose—
One—to taste the hidden flower
of this Life
diving like a bee into its Heart
and surfacing
in all your Bliss—
And One to share the song
of this unfolding,
Carrying the message
of your Sweetness
on my lips.

3

Healing Power of Community in Recovery

Human beings have always lived in community with one another. Only in recent times have human lives become so fragmented as to presume that individuals can live apart from the fabric of community life. Even those who may appear to be living separately are part of an invisible, interdependent web of existence.

As the old adage goes, "No man is an island" (no woman, either!). As human beings, we exist in profound interrelationships—with our multidimensional selves, with one another in community, and with the earth and all creation.

The Buddhist teacher Thich Nhat Hanh has invented a word—interbeing—that describes this quality of interconnectedness. *Interbeing* means being in profound interrelationship with all life.

One of the most powerful healing forces in the recovery process is the healing power of community. By this we are referring

to the complementarity and synergy between one's personal healing and the healing process of others, especially those with whom
one has consistent personal contact.

The field of holistic medicine recognizes that each of us exists
as an interdependent "community" of organs, tissues, cells, molecules, atoms, and subatomic particles—and a mind, body, emotions, and spirit. Although we may seem to be made up of these
different parts, we are healthy and whole only when all these various dimensions of ourselves are communicating and cooperating
effectively.

What use would our lungs be, for example, if it weren't for
the heart to pump the oxygenated blood? The usefulness of our
nervous system would surely be diminished were there no muscles
to respond to the nerve impulses.

Harvard anthropologist Karen Brown studied tribal healing
and its implications for our modern world. In her research, she
pointed out that so-called primitive cultures typically hold the
belief that "when one individual is ill, whether it be a physiological disease or a marital dispute, the results are nearly always
viewed as an illness that affects both the individual and the greater
community."

Given this belief, it is typical in such societies to view the
healing of the individual as inseparable from the healing of the
group. When one person becomes ill, the entire community takes
an active role in the healing process.

The following story highlights the healing potential of living
cooperatively in community. It is adapted from John McNeill's
book, *Taking a Chance on God*.

Heaven and Hell

An old rabbi who was approaching the end of his life
prayed fervently to God that he might be shown the true
nature of heaven and hell. Upon hearing this request, God
appeared in a vision and led the rabbi down a hallway to a

door. Behind the door, the rabbi could hear terrible sounds: moaning, groaning, and mournful, sobbing cries.

When the door was opened, a circle of emaciated human beings could be seen gathered around a huge iron cooking kettle. It was filled to the brim with the most deliciously fragrant stew; and yet, the people looked like skeletons. They were starving to death, even with that sumptuous meal right in front of them.

Everyone at the table had a four-foot-long wooden spoon growing out of each hand. The spoons were much too long for the people to feed themselves, so as they tried to eat, they only grew more and more frustrated and hungry.

"This," God said to the rabbi, "is hell."

Once again, God led the rabbi down the same hallway and brought him to a door that looked identical to the first. But behind this door, the rabbi heard the sounds of laughter and joy. When the door was opened, he saw before him another group of people with the same long wooden appendages growing out of their hands. Yet, they were singing and filled with joy, looking radiantly healthy and alive.

"This," God said, "is heaven."

The difference was that the second group was *feeding one another* with the spoons.

We resonate with the allegorical window on heaven that this little story offers: Heaven (on earth) is when we feed and care for one another so that together we may grow and prosper, in ways that we cannot accomplish on our own. Indeed, we have seen how helping our clients build cooperative community supports them in finding their own "heaven on earth."

The fellowship of AA, Narcotics Anonymous (NA), and other twelve-step groups embodies the essence of community healing, viewing it as a gateway through which the addicted or recovering individual can find a new way of living and being. Aldous Huxley once said that "when all the dust settles from the twentieth century, the formulation of AA and the Twelve Steps will be regarded as one of the century's greatest, most significant social experiments."

The preamble of AA states that "Alcoholics Anonymous is a fellowship of men and women who share their experience, strength and hope with each other so that they may solve their common problems and help others to recover from alcoholism."

AA does, in fact, provide a strong community of outstretched hands and open hearts, a loving community that reaches out to the suffering individual and welcomes her. AA and the Twelve Steps usually use the term "we" rather than "I" as a way of underscoring the interdependent nature of those in recovery.

For AA's several million members worldwide, group meetings are the primary format in which community is fostered. Individuals are encouraged to find a sponsor—a man or a woman well established in sobriety who can assist the newcomer on his fledgling journey of recovery. This sponsor acts as a guide, a partner in healing who helps the newly sober individual work through the steps and become more fully integrated into the fellowship of AA.

Addiction breeds isolation. Once a person enters the portal of recovery, community is a key ingredient in the healing process, so Twelve Steps meetings provide a place for recovering addicts to come together to share stories, successes and failures, joys and struggles. A climate of unconditional love permeates the meetings.

This climate of "radical acceptance" has a profound healing effect upon individuals and for the group itself.

The mystic poet Rumi wrote:

> *There is a community of the spirit.*
> *Join it and feel the delight*
> *of walking in the noisy street,*
> *and being the noise . . .*

Why do you stay in prison
when the door is wide open?
Move outside the tangle of fear-thinking.
Live in silence.
Flow down and down in always
widening rings of being.

AA is not the only way to build community, of course. We also encourage clients to reach out to the human family by participating in support groups of various kinds.

Our experience has been that, in recovery, there is a direct correlation between a client's health and well-being and the depth of her involvement with a strong healing community in which she feels love, intimacy, support, and a deep kinship with others.

In a sermon given by the late Reverend Martin Luther King Jr., an interesting parallel is drawn. In speaking of the giant redwood trees of northern California, King points out that these impressive trees have surprisingly shallow root structures. Yet they still manage to support themselves by interlocking their vast horizontal roots with the roots of other trees, both large and small.

By affirming their mutuality, by linking with the other trees in a sacred web of interdependence, the redwoods can stand tall and be supported. The same holds true for the recovering addict in relation to her community: She can stand tall and find a deep sense of stability through linking up with her community of others.

We typically give our clients in recovery the following suggestions for creating a healing community.

1. *Commit to meeting regularly with a "home group" in AA/NA.* Really get involved in the meetings you attend. Don't be a passive bystander.

2. *Find a sponsor and use that person as a resource.* Choose as your AA/NA sponsor a man or woman for whom you feel an

affinity, someone who has gained a solid foothold in recovery and who can serve as your guide and companion as you journey along your road to recovery.

(Note: Sponsorship is not a panacea. Issues may arise that require outside professional assistance [see below].)

3. *Become involved in service work within AA or in the community at large.* Volunteer at an AA desk hotline, homeless shelter, or hospital addiction treatment center. Take an AA meeting to a prison or hospital, or to an invalid. Reach out! Consider the wisdom in the AA maxim that states that one can *keep* the gift of sobriety only by *freely giving it away* to others.

4. *Find a spiritual director/guide.* A spiritual director can work with you on an ongoing basis to help you develop your spirituality. The process of spiritual direction, or mentoring, is an ancient tradition woven into all the world's great religions. Just as in the business world one might seek a mentor for guidance along the professional path, a spiritual director can serve as a mentor or wise friend whose role is to offer support for one's spiritual development.

Some spiritual directors affiliate with a particular religious denomination, while others do not. What's important is that you choose a spiritual director with whom you are in harmony.

Referrals from friends, your sponsor, or your church, synagogue, or temple may be useful. There are also many certification and training programs throughout the world that can provide referrals. One excellent organization to contact is Spiritual Directors International, 1329 Seventh Ave., San Francisco, CA 94122-2507, (415) 566-1560.

5. *Create or join a men's or women's support group.* We have been part of an active men's group for many years. Along with eight

other men, we have shared many rites of passage—illness, death, marriage and divorce, joys and sorrows. We've found profound healing in a group such as this, where individuals meet for the sole purpose of sharing what is meaningful in their lives. Deep intimacy and a healthy interdependence grows over time.

Same-gender support groups have the added advantage of highlighting shared male experiences or shared female experiences in a safe environment. Community with one's brothers and sisters can be built through the open sharing of those experiences that would not likely be spoken of in the presence of the opposite sex.

Addictive behaviors are typically rooted in shame, including shame about one's sexual expression and identity. These topics are often too "hot" or emotionally loaded to be brought up in the presence of members of the opposite sex.

In same-gender groups, members often discover that what they had secretly felt ashamed of (masturbation, for example) is actually a part of the normal experience of other men and women. Through learning to speak more openly about what had been hidden because of shame, members learn that they are not alone, but rather normal men or women learning ways to make their lives better.

We have found same-gender groups of this kind to be an invaluable resource in the lives of our clients, many of whom are already participating in such a group.

Here are some guidelines for starting a group:

- Find four to eight people to begin a group and commit to meeting at least once a month for a minimum of two hours.
- At the first meeting, make a firm agreement to start and end the group on time.

- Light a candle and keep it lit throughout the meeting as a symbol of the presence of life energy.
- Utilize a "talking stick." This can be any object the group chooses for that purpose—a stone, a stick, a special feather, or something else. Whoever holds the stick "has the floor." The others agree to listen and not interrupt or comment in any way until that member relinquishes the talking stick. Then, another member may pick it up and speak. This format encourages active listening by all group members and keeps intellectualizing or "therapizing" to a minimum.
- The group can plan an agenda, such as the discussion of a particular book or article of general interest to the group. However, we have found that *no agenda at all* is generally best. Without a predetermined agenda superimposed upon the process, whatever needs to be talked about can naturally emerge.

We've found that there's always plenty to discuss, so that the most important ingredients are a commitment to attendance, punctuality, and active participation. We recommend, too, that there be an agreement among group members to honor confidentiality, so that safety and trust can be nurtured.

We have found that diversity is a source of strength and richness for the group. Our own group, for example, includes men whose ages range from their thirties to their seventies, and who are both straight and gay.

6. *Create a crisis intervention/life transition support team.* During a particularly challenging life crisis or transition such as divorce, midlife crisis, career change, or the death of a loved one, it can be helpful to enlist a support team of friends to

accompany you—to energetically hold your hand—during that time of adversity.

Many recovering addicts have a tendency to go it alone, because that has been the only way they've known how to survive. Learning how to receive genuine support from others may not come easily for them. It may require a major shift in perspective from independence/separateness to interdependence.

What's needed is a healthy balance between independence and interdependence—well described by the AA "elder statesman" who said, "I can't do it alone, yet I alone can do it."

Clearly, we flourish best with the support and assistance of others. Here are some guidelines for creating a personal support team:

- Identify one or more close friends whose judgment you trust and with whom you feel safe, people who "have their feet on the ground" and who may be willing to assist you. Contact each of them, discuss the nature of your crisis/transition, and ask if they will serve as part of your support team.
- Ask if they will be on call for you (around the clock, just during the day, only on weekdays, etc.). Make an agreement to check in with each other by telephone or in some other way. This arrangement can be for a specific period of time (a few months, for example), or it can be more open-ended.

Clients often benefit greatly from having a support team of the kind that we are suggesting. They often tell us that the team provided an interpersonal safe haven for them, a place of refuge during turbulent times. Members of the support team themselves typically benefit, too. They often report feeling uplifted by being part of this helping connection.

7. *Find a therapist/therapy group.* Sometimes there's a need for more assistance than friends can provide. In that case, seek out a good counselor/psychotherapist. A referral from a trusted friend, health professional, or clergyman may be a good place to begin.

    Take the time to find someone who is a good match for you. This will be an important (sometimes the most important!) relationship in your life. Treat it as such.

Ultimately, community is built one relationship at a time—that is, by strengthening each relationship one has by *caring enough* about it, investing the time and energy that it warrants.

Here's an exercise that can help you build an intimate bridge with another human being. This is a focusing exercise that can be of benefit in any situation where you care enough about a relationship to want to improve it.

This focusing exercise can be especially useful to the recovering addict in his quest to build healthy relationships in the present and to make amends for past actions and attitudes that may have created pain for himself and for others.

Building an Intimate Bridge

These days, many people have problems with intimacy. It doesn't feel safe to them to get close to others. They feel out of touch, cut off from the world.

Particularly in relationships where intimacy is most desirable—in marriages and other primary relationships, for example—something gets in the way of intimate connection. It may feel as though the partners are in opposite corners of the same room, breathing different air from seemingly separate universes.

Our breath is the most intimate connection we have with the world around us. As we breathe, the outside world is taken in as molecules of oxygen and nitrogen. The air containing these molecules passes through our nostrils or mouth, then into a series of branching tubes leading to our lungs, and ultimately to—and through—our heart.

The breath moves between us and the surrounding environment, giving no real clue about where the boundary lies. Where exactly does "out there" stop and become part of "us"? Where does our own "inside" begin?

There is no clear dividing line. Through the breath, we are fully exposed to the life that is all around us. We cannot avoid this intimacy. We all breathe the same air.

As we breathe, our inside and our outside form a continuum. By focusing on our breathing, by noticing its seamless quality, we create deeper intimacy with ourselves and with our living environment.

If you want to feel more connected and at home with someone, try this exercise to help clear the air of any impediments that may exist between you:

Close your eyes and visualize that person sitting across from you, mirroring your posture. Notice that she (we use the feminine pronoun here, so substitute he/his, if appropriate) has a benevolent look on her face and is openly receptive to being with you.

Notice her chest gently rising and falling. She is breathing the very same air as you, and you recognize that it is perfectly healthy and safe to share the same air with her.

Feel and see the air passing from her left nostril, out into the space between you, and then into your left nostril. The air now moves into your chest, where it is purified by passing through your heart.

You breathe this purified air out through your right nostril, out into the air space between the two of you, and back into your "breathing mate's" right nostril, whereupon she allows the air to pass through her chest and heart, then back out again through her left nostril toward you, as the cycle repeats itself.

The path of the breath between you and your breathing partner takes the shape of a figure eight, the symbol of infinity. Here, as you breathe in unison, it signifies the unlimited depth of connection that is possible between you.

If your breathing partner is agreeable, this exercise can also be done with her actually sitting across from you.

Each relationship presents us with an infinite range of possibilities. When we actively choose to "breathe the same air" in tandem with one another and in communion with the Living Spirit, we join together with all living beings in our earth community.

A Community of Helpers

Expect your every need to be met,
expect the answer to every problem,
expect abundance on every level.

—Eileen Caddy

One of the most virulent stressors in these modern times is the perception that we are all alone, that time is short. There is so much to do, so little time!

This perception creates a state of inner tension, which tends to be associated with a sense of isolation. Many individuals begin the day with a list of tasks that is not humanly possible to accomplish.

With many of our clients in recovery, we see a tendency not only to feel alone but also to overdo, in the spirit of trying to make up for lost time—especially when they are first entering recovery. It is as if the flame of rebirth has been turned up so high, and the desire to live life with intensity and passion has become so great, that the pot is nearly boiling over with good intention and high motivation.

> **Ironically, that newfound drive to somehow make up for what has been missed can itself become a significant relapse factor, particularly when the individual "over-shoots the target" and begins to pursue unrealistic goals.**

For example, several of our clients, still in their twenties and thirties, became nearly obsessed with the idea of catching up in order to make up for lost time with their college studies. This misguided enthusiasm led them to sign up for more classes in one semester than was realistic. In so doing, they set themselves up for almost inevitable failure.

Another client, whose personality type was the typical rescuer often found in ACOA (adult children of alcoholics) circles, began her own secondhand clothing business almost immediately after becoming sober. At the same time, she was continuing to raise her three children and to maintain the home where she and her family lived. She also began to pursue a master's degree in social work. All this proved to be too much for her to manage. In her misguided attempt to "do it all," she ultimately drove herself to relapse and to the brink of despair.

One expression of this "island consciousness" that characterizes many individuals in recovery (and many nonaddicts, as well) is the well-intentioned practice of making a daily to-do list—which is then used in a self-defeating way. We are talking here about a daily list of demands or reminders that an individual constructs early in the day in order to delineate all the tasks that she *must* accomplish before the day is over.

If you're at all typical, you make a to-do list in which you ask way too much of yourself. By the end of the day, there's probably a lot left undone—and there's not likely to have been much feeling of satisfaction or accomplishment along the way, either. You're more likely to have noticed what's *not* been accomplished than what has.

> **For our clients in recovery, we recommend a different kind of to-do list that allows them to liberate themselves from the bondage of those overwhelming, self-abusive lists and the unrealistic demands that underlie them.**

With this method, our client learns to *consciously choose* what she *really* intends to accomplish that day through her own efforts—and to *intentionally delegate* what's left to a team of helpers.

We encourage each individual to set realistic priorities based upon personal preference. She can then choose tasks that she is genuinely prepared to take on and delegate to her team anything she'd like them to work on.

We call this approach "The Placemat Technique," so named because its creators are said to have used the back of a placemat (at a restaurant where they were having breakfast) to make their first list. We learned it from a student of Abraham (a wise teacher who speaks through Esther Hicks—please see page 221 in the Resources section for information about her publications and Web site).

Here's how it works. You may want to take out a sheet of paper right now and give it a try.

The Placemat Technique

1. Take a moment to center yourself.

2. Draw a vertical line down the middle of a sheet of paper.

3. List "Things I plan to do today" on the left side of the page. (An important reminder: List only those items that you feel committed to investing your energy in, those that you *really*

intend to accomplish that day, not those you think you "should" do!)

4. On the right side of the page, list those things that you'd like your "helpers" or "The Universe" to work on. These are items that are important to you, too, but that you're not yet ready to invest your energy in or take action on right now; for example, "finding money for that vacation trip to the ocean" or "making contact with someone who can advise me on how to use natural pesticides on my garden," or even more mundane items like "getting the food shopping done" or "getting Sara to her music lesson."

5. Proceed with your day. Focus on tackling the items that you've listed to the left of the vertical line. And just let your helpers—to whom you've given instruction on what you want/need them to do by what you've written to the right of the line—work their magic!

We've discovered that "The Universe" does indeed work in wonderful, serendipitous ways, whenever one is willing to go public *by stating a clear intention and giving specific direction.*

> **Whenever we're willing to say—*specifically*—what we want, while staying open to the logistics of how that might happen, results often come "as if by magic" in ways that we might never have imagined.**

Here's a real-life example of the power of naming what you want: One Saturday morning, Barry listed "getting the yard looking neat and well manicured" on his "Placemat To-Do List" as something for his helpers to work on. Ten minutes later, a friendly neighbor of his stopped by with an electric hedge clipper that he'd just acquired. Eager to show off his new toy, he smilingly offered to give a demonstration. He then proceeded—

with great enthusiasm and skill!—to trim all the yew and for-sythia bushes that border Barry's yard.

By upgrading your method of making to-do lists in the way that we've suggested, you invite yourself to dance co-creatively with all the forces in play, even though you may not know what they are or who they may be. You enlist the support of your helper angels by your willingness to ask for what you want!

Whether these helpers (visible or invisible) are actually out there or whether they're really inside you as heretofore untapped parts of yourself doesn't really matter. The practical result is the same: Harsh, unrealistic demands become upgraded to "soft pref-erences" about what one can realistically accomplish.

> **Intentionally working with invisible helpers activates a sense of community-in-action, a healthy alternative to the "island consciousness" that often plagues the recov-ering addict.**

In Community with the Natural World

The union of human nature
and Great Nature
is the ground
from which all healthy relationships grow

—John Milton

An issue that often troubles the recovering addict is the whole question of acceptance; namely, "Do I belong here? Am I wel-come?" Clients in recovery frequently describe themselves as feel-ing isolated and alone, cut off from the source of life.

Indeed, one of the most common traits of addicts is this sense of alienation and isolation. As AA co-founder Bill Wilson has written in *The Twelve Steps and The Twelve Traditions,* one of the gifts of recovery is "reclaiming a *deep and profound sense of belonging* as a man or woman who no longer feels that (s)he is living in a hostile world."

Addiction treatment centers are seldom equipped to deal with this existential loneliness; yet, we see recovery as a form of *rebirth* that asks individuals to learn new ways of reconnecting with all aspects of life as they reclaim their bodies, minds, emotions, and spirits in sobriety.

One of the most direct and powerful ways that we've discovered for an individual to resolve this existential angst in favor of feeling received by life is to actively engage with the natural world. Something as simple as going for a walk in the woods, meandering along a river or stream, or sitting quietly under an oak tree in a meadow can offer profound solace and friendly companionship to anyone who may be feeling out of the loop of life.

Connecting with nature on a regular basis can be a rich and simple way for the recovering addict to discover potent truths about life and about herself.

Michael Cohen's book *Re-Connecting with Nature* offers many tips for engaging the natural world that can be useful for those in recovery. Through activities like those described by Cohen, recovering addicts develop a sense of reverence for the natural world, learn to listen attentively to nature's voice, and feel welcomed by the plants and trees, embraced by beauty, and at home in nature's sanctuary.

4

Tools for Staying Steady in an Unsteady World

For anyone in recovery—and for anyone working with or related to someone in recovery—the capacity to hold steady, to stay calm in the midst of stress-inducing challenges is an ability well worth cultivating. Indeed, the success of the recovery process is often predicated upon the recovering addict's ability to effectively manage life's vicissitudes as they occur, over and over again. The techniques offered in this chapter can be used to weather those inevitable storms—to stay afloat, no matter how large the waves may be.

Modern living continues to become more and more intense. The ongoing experience of feeling nearly overwhelmed by stress can be disabling—even deadly—for addict and nonaddict alike. This incessant, malignant stress is at the core of many chronic diseases, including alcoholism and other addictions.

Not only are the tools discussed in this chapter helpful in a variety of situations, but *making the choice to use them* is, in itself, steadying and empowering. In other words, each tool provides a specific benefit, and there is also a general benefit that is common to all three—the "perk," if you will, of strengthening one's confidence through the very process of taking charge, of "doing something" by taking effective action.

In taking charge proactively, a cognitive shift occurs in which the angst of feeling like a victim (that is, of feeling at the mercy of the vagaries of life) becomes replaced by a feeling of peace and steadiness associated with feeling in charge, as the author of one's own life story.

Reclaiming "authorship" of one's own life can be a very powerful step toward successful recovery from addictions.

Stop, Look, Listen, and Choose

Here is a focusing/reframing exercise that can be used any time things are not going the way you want. This cognitive technique provides an easy avenue for working consciously and co-creatively with your innate capacity for change.

By practicing this exercise you will make an *inner shift* that naturally leads you to correct your course. By changing the way you *perceive* things, you change your *experience* of what is going on. That naturally leads to less stress, and to healthier, more empowered action.

At first, it may take you several minutes to complete this, but you will find that as you practice and become more familiar with the steps, you'll be able to do it very quickly, probably in half a minute or less.

Life sometimes has moments that are problematic. At those times, we may find ourselves at a crossroads. This is something like approaching a railroad crossing, where a speeding train is about to barrel on through. If we choose to, we can stop, look, listen, and judiciously pause—so that we will not be hit broadside by the approaching train!

Here, the speeding train represents an old habit, an old way of processing information that has led to distressed feelings and thoughts, time and time again. But we needn't continue to be run over—or overwhelmed—by these old habitual ways that no longer serve us.

In this exercise, you utilize your capacity to stop, look, listen, pause, and then *choose* the path that you truly desire. You can use this approach anytime you want to change course, whenever things are not going the way you want them to and you find yourself thinking and behaving on automatic.

> **This cognitive exercise is a way of using your power of choice/intention to strategically redirect the course of your life at any moment.**

Whenever you find yourself at a crossroads, whenever there's some glitch in your day where things are not going so well, when you're feeling frustrated, overwhelmed, out of control, remember that you are the one who calls the shots. You're the one who's in charge!

1. **Stop.** Call "time out." "Blow the whistle." If you like, make the letter *T* with your hands as if you were the referee of your own "game of life" (which, of course, you are!).

   Remind yourself that there are many options other than "being on automatic" with old patterns of behavior and thought. The way you've been proceeding in the past is *not* the only way to go. There are many other possibilities!

2. **Look.** Take a candid, honest look at what's going on. Ask yourself, "What's going on here?" Answer that question by

giving yourself a brief "news report" (include the news of what's going on inside of you as well as externally).

For example, "Well . . . what's going on is that I am feeling tired and irritable. I'm stuck in traffic and I'm feeling anxious about being late for the meeting."

3. **Listen.** Feel your feet, especially the bottoms of your feet (as described in detail on page 53). Feel the earth underneath you. Bring your awareness to the feeling of contact that the soles of your feet make with the earth (the floor, etc.).

Now bring your attention to your chest, especially to the area in the center of your chest near your heart. (You don't have to be anatomically precise. Anywhere in the general vicinity of your heart will do.)

This is a way of affirming your willingness to listen to the heart's wisdom and hearing what it may have to say. It is a way of listening "deeper," past the rational mind, to a place in you that knows the truth about what you *really* want.

Notice the feeling is in your chest, in whatever way you may sense this. Ask yourself, "What do I *really* want?" Then, answer that question for yourself, letting what you *feel* in your chest guide you. This is your way of finding out what is genuinely your heart's desire, right in that moment.

4. **Choose.** Construct a one-sentence choice for what you want and how you want to be feeling/experiencing the situation that you're in. Begin with the words "I choose to enjoy." (For example, "I choose to enjoy feeling balanced and at ease right now, feeling confident that I will arrive at the meeting at just the right time.")

This choice reflects what you really want, right here, right now.

5. **Let it go!** Now, just forget about it. Proceed with your day. This letting go is an essential step in the process. You've done your work! Now just release it and let it be.

> **What you have effectively done, to use a golfing analogy, is to retrieve your ball from the rough and, ever so gently, place it on the fairway (of life) again.**

You might want to take a moment now to thank yourself for caring enough about you to be willing to explore new ways of being that can be more enjoyable and that can free you from old habits that have been less than optimal for getting you where you *really* want to go.

Acknowledge yourself for being willing to experiment with these new ways—for being an intrepid pioneer of Inner Space!

The Secret

In this exercise, which we call "The Secret," you learn to calm and center yourself by using the power of your imagination. Please note that in this exercise, no effort is required. Here you're not trying to breathe more deeply or to make yourself calm. For the recovering addict who may at times be overcompensating—trying too hard to make changes happen—this exercise may be an excellent antidote to his well-intentioned, yet misdirected efforts to make things right!

Each time you take a breath, you welcome and receive oxygen into your lungs. From there, the oxygen becomes distributed throughout the body by way of the bloodstream.

This life-sustaining oxygen is carried by a system of "roadways" that vary in size from major "highways" called arteries to smaller "byways" called arterioles and capillaries. The oxygen that travels along these pathways brings life to all your cells.

By using your imagination, you can magnify the efficiency of this oxygen transport system. You can play a powerful role in enhancing your own vitality and becoming centered and calm.

All you need to know is this secret about yourself:

You have a unique anatomy, known only to yourself. Your lungs are located in your belly, right behind your navel.

By *imagining* that you have secret lungs in your belly that no one else knows about, you will *automatically* breathe more deeply.

Try it right now. Imagine that your lungs are in your belly. Feel them comfortably nestled in behind your navel, with plenty of room to expand and contract. Enjoy this feeling for a few moments, or for as long as you wish.

Check in with your lungs from time to time during the day and just make sure that you are breathing into them. See and feel the breath of life traveling there, carrying life-giving oxygen to exactly where it needs to go. By practicing this simple exercise in imagination, you can effectively support yourself in living a calm and vital life.

Connecting with the Earth

The real miracle
is not to walk
either on water
or in thin air
but to walk
on earth

—Thich Nhat Hanh

Conventional AA wisdom admonishes us, "Don't just do something . . . Stand there!" In reality, none of us can avoid connecting with the earth: We are all pulled by earth's gravity, at all times. However, by *consciously* connecting with the earth, that is, by directing our attention to the part of us that generally makes the most direct contact with the earth—namely, our feet—we can steady and center ourselves at any moment that we choose.

This is an exercise in feeling the feet with one's awareness. For most people, the feet are an emotionally neutral part of the body, so there is generally little resistance or hesitation in focusing there. The feet are also farthest away from the head, which is the natural home of our thought processes, the focal point of our thinking. Consequently, focusing on the feet helps us balance out the mind chatter that tends to dominate our awareness and that often promotes anxiety and worry.

Right now, take a comfortable sitting position with your eyes either open or closed, whichever is more comfortable for you. Thank yourself for your willingness to explore the potential benefits that might be available for you in this exercise.

Now, allow yourself to begin to "touch your feet with your awareness." Bring your attention to your feet and notice anything that is true in this moment about how your feet feel.

You may experience the feeling in your feet as a warmth or a tingling, or as a sense of heaviness or fullness. Just notice whatever you feel.

What's helpful in this exercise is when you simply pay attention to whatever is true for you, right now. There is no right or wrong way to do this. There is nothing right or wrong to feel.

> Notice whether it's easier to feel one foot more than the other . . . or do they feel about the same? Can you feel your toes?

Now, let yourself become especially aware of the feeling in the bottoms of your feet . . . the feeling of gentle pressure that the soles of your feet make with the floor.

The earth is supporting your feet. Even if you were to let go of all the tension in your feet, the earth would still support them. See if you can get a sense of this: your feet supported by the earth, the floor under your feet like a steady platform, always there for you, offering support.

And now, gently bring your attention back to the surroundings in the room. Softly open your eyes (if your eyes were closed). Become aware of the chair or couch you are sitting on.

Notice how you feel right now.

If there's any way that you feel different (more calm, more steady and centered), just realize that you did it! *You* made that change by your willingness and choice to consciously feel your feet and your connection with the earth.

You may also practice feeling your feet during odd moments such as standing in line at the grocery store or bank, waiting at a stoplight, or taking a walk. Especially feel the soles of your feet making contact with the floor, sidewalk, or ground as you walk.

Energy follows attention. By shifting some of your attention into (the soles of) your feet, you will automatically become calmer, as excess energy moves out of the thinking brain and becomes more grounded in the earth.

5

Prayer and Meditation in Recovery

The seed of God is in us.
Now
the seed of a pear tree
grows into a pear tree
and a hazel seed
grows into a hazel tree;
the seed of God is in us—
a seed of God
grows into God.

—Meister Eckhart

Prayer and meditation are two of the most powerful and effective approaches to healthy living that we know. These spiritual disciplines are particularly relevant for the recovering addict who may desperately need to reconnect with his core essence as a foundation for regaining healthy balance in his life.

We regularly utilize the healing power of prayer and meditation in our clinical practices and in our personal lives and have found them to be extraordinarily useful in the healing work we do with people who are recovering from all kinds of addictions.

We want to make these approaches accessible and acceptable to you. Thus, our intention is to present these topics in a way that will help demystify them and dispel any misconceptions that could dissuade you from utilizing prayer and meditation in the recovery process.

What do we mean by prayer? For our purposes, we define prayer as any action, either inner or outer, that one chooses in order to connect with a power greater than oneself.

And what do we mean by meditation? Meditation is a deliberate practice of focusing the mind in order to achieve a heightened awareness of who one really is, as well as to have an experience of deep relaxation.

Clearly, these two practices are somewhat overlapping. They are difficult to describe in words, because both are highly experiential and personal. To attain the benefits, you must practice.

In order to more fully understand what prayer and meditation can make possible for you and for those whom you seek to assist, you have to "be there."

Individuals in recovery are often very self-absorbed. This is understandable, of course, given the life-or-death nature of the challenge facing them. But self-absorption in the extreme can be counterproductive. An individual can become locked into health-destroying patterns of belief and action, and yet be totally unaware of it. This blindness to one's own health-destroying ideas and habits is often seen in recovering addicts.

Prayer and meditation can provide a doorway out of this cubicle of self-absorption, thereby initiating the recovering addict into a transpersonal realm that is bigger than himself—a realm of peace and serenity where a deeper understanding of his true nature becomes possible.

Thus, the twin practices of prayer and meditation can be of great benefit to those on the recovery path. At times, they can be lifesaving!

Prayer is one way that the recovering addict can make a deliberate, conscious choice to place herself more fully in the presence of the sacred, to emerge from the clutter of her ego-centered mind, and dive deeply into the part of herself that is beyond divisions or distinctions. She can enter a place where she can begin to feel at one with her deepest self and with the universe in which she dwells.

We view prayer and meditation as soul sisters, twin springs that emanate from one Divine Source. These practices help us connect with our innate capacity to heal. Through meditation and prayer, we can contact that place in our hearts where we can rest in the presence of the sacred and feel at peace. We can come home.

> **Heartfelt prayer is a potent means of invoking healing energy into our own lives and into the lives of those for whom we pray. Genuine prayer penetrates the very marrow of our souls.**

When we connect to this Divine Source within, we become more powerful ourselves. We can then more easily transcend the obstacles that might have threatened our well-being—and our sobriety—in the past.

Step 2 of the Twelve Steps of AA states, "We came to believe that a power greater than ourselves could restore us to sanity."

Prayer and meditation are avenues through which an individual can directly access her "sanity" by contacting a power that is herself, yet is greater than herself (a paradox!). She may call that power God, humanity, spirit; or he may give it some other name.

What really matters is not the name but the recovering addict's *recognition* that there is a power greater than herself—a power that she can tap into regularly, anytime she chooses.

Prayer and meditation can thereby be used by the recovering addict to effectively support a process of self-liberation. By surrendering in a healthy way to the power of one's addiction (by this we don't mean giving up one's power to change, but rather acknowledging that addiction is indeed a formidable foe!), the recovering addict can begin to open a doorway to freedom.

Bill Wilson, one of AA's co-founders, pondered the scope of spiritual awakening when he wrote: "Is sobriety all that we are to expect of a spiritual awakening? No, sobriety is only a bare beginning; it is the first gift of the first awakening. If more gifts are to be received, our awakening has to go on."

In keeping with that perspective, we view prayer and meditation as magnificent instruments, living tools for helping individuals in recovery to awaken and grow.

We will present a variety of prayers and meditations that we've found to be easily accessible and acceptable to those of different faiths. As pragmatic mystics, we hope to show you how prayer and meditation may serve as invaluable, practical tools for living a healthy life in sobriety.

> *Look to this day,*
> *for it is life,*
> *the very life of life.*
> *In its brief course lie all*
> *the realities and verities of existence,*
> *the bliss of growth,*
> *the splendor of action,*
> *the glory of power.*

For yesterday is but a dream,
and tomorrow is only a vision,
but today, well lived,
makes every yesterday
a dream of happiness
and every tomorrow
a vision of hope.
Look well therefore, to this day.

—Hindu proverb

Each day we've been allotted our twenty-four hours to live. This gift of life is both precious and tentative. We all know how suddenly that gift can be snatched away by the seemingly wanton vagaries of fate.

Everything is present right here—the possibility of achieving peace, of attaining wholeness, of knowing God. The challenge facing the individual in recovery is how to stay in touch with and truly partake of this golden opportunity that is always available in this present moment.

Prayer and meditation can be vital tools for learning how to live more fully in the only moment we ever have—the present moment. This present moment is a holy moment, a healing moment, for every breath and every step we take has the potential for being a moment of peace, joy, and serenity.

The way we see it, recovery is a journey that can be deliciously enhanced by judicious, yet bold experimentation with new ways of living and being. Yet, many people in recovery, in particular those who may feel a disaffinity for religion, may ask, "Why bother with such things?" They wonder if prayer and meditation are really useful or necessary.

One example is Milton, a client who recalls an essential shift of attitude that he experienced while in recovery, one that allowed him to become open to the healing benefits of prayer. At the time, he was just out of rehabilitation and was very antagonistic to religion. He thought of himself as agnostic and would bristle at the word "God."

Although he had learned to meditate, Milton vehemently eschewed prayer, which was anathema to him because he associated it with religion. One day his AA sponsor suggested that he experiment with prayer by literally getting down on his knees and asking the universe to help him stay sober. This would not constitute religion. Rather, it would be his own personal plea for help, affirming his willingness to receive assistance from wherever it might come.

Even though he was embarrassed by the very thought of being seen praying to "some God I don't believe in" (he recalls barricading his room by placing a chair against the door to avoid being caught in the act), he was nonetheless willing to try it. Milton discovered that when he did pray in this manner, a deep feeling of peace and connectedness ensued. Being a results-oriented person, he was impressed enough by what had occurred to continue experimenting with prayer on a more regular basis.

We have found over the years that prayer and meditation can be quite effective tools for assisting men and women in recovery in a variety of ways, including:

- helping them manage withdrawal symptoms, such as insomnia, agitation, panic attacks, and other emotional states typically associated with early stages of recovery.
- helping them lower blood pressure and normalize heart rate, especially during early stages of recovery when the highly stressed nervous system is trying to come back into balance.
- providing them an ongoing mechanism for expanding self-awareness and achieving peace of mind.

- helping them find greater meaning and connection with themselves, with others, and with all of life.

In general, we've found that utilizing prayer and meditation as part of one's path to healing in recovery invokes the following qualities:

• serenity	• wisdom
• faith	• gratitude
• personal freedom	• humility
• trust	• hope
• love	• joy
• understanding	• a feeling of security
• compassion	• presence

As we set out now to explore more fully the specific benefits of prayer and meditation in recovery, we want to share these core beliefs of ours, to establish a context for what follows:

1. We believe that there is a source of divine energy, or God, within everyone. There are many names for this sacred energy, all of which are appropriate "names of God." Step 3 of AA uses the wording: "God *as we understand Him*" (italics ours). What is implied in this phrase is that it is our individual responsibility and choice to define God, or Sacred Energy, however we understand that Presence to be, in our own particular way.

2. There are many ways to pray and to meditate. We view all of them as valid, as long as they are useful and effective for the individual.

There are no right or wrong ways to pray or to meditate. Whatever works, works!

We do, however, encourage personal experimentation to see what's best for you. Be creative!

Prayers for Healing in Recovery

God's Wounds

Through the great pain of stretching
beyond all that pain has taught me,
the soft well at the base
has opened, and life
touching me there
has turned me into a flower
that prays for rain. Now
I understand: to blossom
is to pray, to wilt and shed
is to pray, to turn to mulch
is to pray, to stretch in the dark
is to pray, to break the surface
after great months of ice
is to pray, and to squeeze love
up the stalky center towards the sky
with only dreams of color
is to pray, and finally to unfold
again as if never before
is to be the prayer.

—Mark Nepo, *A Waterfall of Hands*

This poem by contemporary American poet Mark Nepo expresses an open-ended and widely inclusive view of what it means to pray that resonates with our own perspectives. We have already defined prayer as any action, either inner or outer, that one chooses to take in order to connect with a power greater than oneself. Here we see that just by being authentically who we are, as always imperfect works in progress, we become living prayers.

Like the plant that's been underground through the long winter before it finally breaks the surface to reach toward the light, a human being, too, is on a journey of growth, maturation, and then eventual decline and death, before the time for recycling comes again. Along the way, her actions and thoughts can be prayers, her dreams and imaginings can be prayers, and her victories both great and small can be prayers—as long as they are linked at some level (either consciously or not) with the intention to know and to connect more fully with that "power greater than herself."

> One's choice to continue living rather than to give up on life, to be willing to move ahead boldly through all of life's unraveling phases, through all the struggles and the victories that may come, is itself a very potent prayer—a prayer to "unfold again as if never before."

This transformative prayer can also be viewed as an affirmation of intention. Here, one fervently declares, "I choose for life!" This choice for life can be the foundation for positive change, a source of strength and of genuine hope, especially at times when the force of destructive habits may feel insurmountable.

The great challenge for the recovering addict, though, is to learn to focus his prayers more consciously on the particular results that he truly desires from the depth of his being, and to trust that those soul-yearnings will benefit him royally as they lead him along the path of sobriety.

> Recovery itself is a homecoming journey, a kind of pilgrimage to one's own heart and soul. On the odyssey of personal transformation, focused prayer is one way to set one's course by pointing in the direction of home.

As we see it, effective prayer is a legitimate and potent healing practice, one that can be exquisitely helpful to the recovering
addict. The eleventh step of AA's Twelve Steps and Traditions offers
this wise perspective on the healing benefits of prayer:

> Those of us who have come to make regular use of prayer
> would no more do without it than we would refuse air, food
> or sunshine. And for the same reason, when we refuse air,
> light or food, the body suffers. And when we turn away
> from prayer and meditation, we likewise deprive our minds,
> our emotions and our intuitions of vitally needed support.
> As the body can fail its purpose for lack of nourishment, so
> can the soul.
>
> There is a direct linkage among self-examination,
> meditation, and prayer. Taken separately, these practices can
> bring much relief and benefit. But when they are logically
> related and interwoven, the result is an unshakable
> foundation for life.

In the discussion that follows, we'll be sharing some prayers
that we've found to be accessible and highly useful vehicles for
traveling recovery's roadway.

First, here are a few guidelines and suggestions:

1. Find a quiet place to pray, one where you can be present with
   yourself and as free from noise and distraction as possible.

2. When offering a prayer, let it unfold from the heart. As you
   pray, allow yourself to feel, *and actively resonate with,* the heartfelt intention that underlies the content of your prayer. (A colleague of ours told us that he sometimes has to say a prayer
   several times before he feels a connection on a heart level with
   its true spirit. So often our minds seek to dominate. Prayer,
   especially when it is heartfelt, can be a way of entering the
   deeper recesses of our being, beyond the mind's purview.)

3. Say the words either silently or aloud and remember to proceed slowly, so that the essence of the prayer can naturally percolate through you. Remember: There is no urgency in Spirit! With prayer, there is nothing to hurry toward.

4. Use nonspecific prayer, that is, prayer directed toward the best possible outcome rather than a specified result, whenever that feels consistent with your intention to be of the highest service. With nonspecific prayer, one practices letting go of any attachment to the specific result, trusting that whatever is for the highest good will, in the fullest sense, be best. This is not necessarily easy to do (naturally, we tend to get invested in specific positive outcomes!), but nonspecific prayer is, in our experience, the most effective form of prayer, as well as being the most respectful of all concerned. It is, therefore, the one we prefer.

Prayer is a means of connecting with the sacred. It deserves to be honored as such.

In twelve-step programs two of the most frequently used prayers are the Serenity Prayer and the Prayer of St. Francis. We've found that these prayers provide a potent foundation for living a sober, free, and joyful life.

The Serenity Prayer

God grant me the serenity
to accept the things I cannot change,
the courage to change the things I can,
and the wisdom to know the difference.

This prayer, frequently recited at the end of twelve-step meetings, is one of the most useful and powerful prayers we know. In essence, it provides a strategy for dealing with challenges, and a clarification of the human and the divine domains. (For those whose beliefs preclude the use of the word "God," we suggest omitting that word from the prayer.)

The Serenity Prayer is like a laser. It can cut through inner confusion and help bring into clearer focus the forces that underlie one's power to change, delineating them from other factors that are simply beyond one's control. By making this distinction, one is better prepared to take strategic action, based upon a more complete awareness and acceptance of whatever life situation one may be facing.

The Serenity Prayer can provide welcome clarity regarding the appropriate next step through an honest assessment of present reality. An experience of serenity is the natural by-product of this more enlightened and balanced acceptance of things just as they are.

Here's one clinical example of the usefulness of the Serenity Prayer. George, a client of ours, had relapsed after two years of sobriety and was in the midst of overwhelming guilt and shame for having "backtracked and fallen off the wagon." We urged him to recite the Serenity Prayer regularly, especially in situations where he had been wallowing in unnecessary and counter-productive self-judgment.

We helped George recognize that though he could not change the fact of his having relapsed, he *could* learn to muster his courage and strength by choosing to admit his mistake (as neutrally as possible, as a kind of "news report" to himself), and then honestly tell both his therapist and his AA compatriots what had taken place. That way, he could gain from his experience and grow stronger, rather than digging himself deeper into a pit of self-loathing.

George agreed to read and recite the Serenity Prayer several times a day. He reported that he felt deeply comforted and a greater sense of peace whenever he did so. Our client discovered that the Serenity Prayer helped him accept more fully the nature of his relapse and provided him with a foundation for looking more deeply into himself, examining in a healthier, more detached way the factors that had contributed to his relapse. By "resetting his sights" in this way, he could begin to make some much-needed changes in his life, including a revised picture of his own worth and abilities.

When we utilize the Serenity Prayer, we learn to accept reality more fully, *just as it is*. We come to know our limits. We begin to choose more wisely the steps that are needed to get our lives back on track.

We can then take judicious actions out in the world, actions that are truly life-enhancing, as we cultivate serenity as part of our inner landscape.

The St. Francis Prayer

Lord, make me an instrument of thy peace—
that where there is hatred, I may bring love—
that where there is wrong, I may bring the spirit of forgiveness—
where there is discord, I may bring harmony—
where there is error, I may bring truth—
where there is doubt, I may bring faith—
where there is despair, I may bring hope—
where there are shadows, I may bring light—
where there is sadness, I may bring joy.
Lord, grant that I may seek rather to comfort than to be
*   comforted—*

to understand than to be understood—
to love, than to be loved.
For it is by self-forgetting that one finds.
It is by forgiving that one is forgiven.
It is by dying that one awakens to Eternal Life.

This prayer has special relevance for anyone in recovery, inasmuch as every recovering addict must die to her addiction in order to walk freely the path of eternal life in sobriety. Through *self-less-ness* (that is, by withdrawing an investment in the small self and reinvesting that energy in higher ideals), anyone can discover more of her true nature and find a deepened sense of meaning.

Years ago, while teaching a course on addiction, Roger had transcribed the St. Francis Prayer onto the blackboard. Looking at what he had written, he had a moment of insight in which he saw that this prayer described perfectly the process of addiction and recovery as he had come to know it. He noticed that if he drew a line down the middle of the blackboard, the prayer became divided into two distinct parts.

The words that appeared on the left-hand side now described the characteristics of addiction, while the qualities of recovery and new life appeared on the right:

Addiction	*Recovery*
Hatred	Love
Wrong	Forgiveness
Discord	Harmony
Error	Truth
Doubt	Faith
Despair	Hope
Shadows	Light
Sadness	Joy

Looked at in this way, the process of recovery can clearly be seen as a healing process in which a former addict recovers within himself the qualities listed under "Recovery," namely, love, forgiveness, harmony, and so on.

Our experience with the St. Francis Prayer is that its words invoke profound healing energy. Saying this prayer while focusing slowly on each word can bring immediate relief to anyone who is suffering, regardless of the cause. When we recite this prayer, we are in essence making a choice to invite the healing energy of balance and equanimity into our lives. We affirm our intention to be of the greatest service to all.

We do encourage creativity! For example, instead of the word "Lord," one may substitute whatever word best reflects one's personal preference. An example of such creativity was displayed by a former client of ours who was uncomfortable reciting the Lord's Prayer. She could not bring herself to refer to God as Father/He. Karen salvaged the value of the prayer for herself by changing "our Father" to "our Father/Mother."

She also added one more letter that upgraded the prayer, changing its meaning to something totally acceptable to her. She changed the words "Hallowed be Thy Name" to "Hallowed be thy names." With this modification, she was now able to feel the prayer as inclusive of her faith in the God-*dess* and in all expressions of the divine, not limited by gender.

An individual in recovery once said: "My will and God's will would be one and the same—if only I had all the facts."

Of course, in life we never have all the facts, nor do we have all the answers. We must bow in humility to the Unknown. Yet, through prayer, we can align ourselves with the "God-force" (or, to use the more secular lingo from the *Star Wars* films, "The Force") within us. This higher power is a force that is much bigger than we are and yet, in a paradoxical way, it is the very same as we.

In our clinical practices, we light a candle at the beginning of each workday and leave it burning throughout the day. Through this candle-lighting ritual, we become more aligned with our own choice to be of the highest and most effective service to our clients. We ask that God's Light and Love flow through the room and into the hearts and minds of each person who comes into our office. The burning flame throughout the day is a reminder to us of our dedication to be of service. It is also a symbol to our clients of the unending availability of life energy.

A Prayer for Healing for the Health Practitioner

I pray that I receive the healing, the guidance, and the strength necessary for my soul's journey.

or

I pray that (the client, John, Sarah, etc.) receive the healing, guidance, and strength necessary for his/her soul's journey.

We say this prayer either silently or aloud each time a client leaves our office. Since we can never know completely what is best for another human being on her soul's journey, we pray that each person we work with (and thus care about!) receive whatever she needs to live a whole and vibrant life. As we recite this prayer, we take a few moments to connect with the Source, asking for the highest good for all while letting go of any "attachment" we may have to the results of our interventions.

Morning Prayer for the Health Practitioner

This prayer can be spoken while kneeling with palms open, if that is in keeping with your beliefs and comfort level. (Kneeling is a humbling posture that brings one closer to the earth and enhances one's receptivity.) It can also be said while standing or sitting.

> *Gracious Spirit, I offer my life into your loving care. I turn my will over to you and pray that you will help keep me clean, clear, and sober in my thoughts and actions. I pray that your Divine Light and Love will illuminate my path today, guiding and sustaining me with every breath I take and every step I make on this sacred planet Earth.*

Buddhist Prayer of Lovingkindness

> *May I be at peace,*
> *May my heart remain open,*
> *May I awaken to the light of my own true nature,*
> *May I be healed,*
> *May I be a source of healing for all beings.*

This healing prayer can be recited for oneself or for a loved one, by substituting his name for "I" and "his" for "my."

It can be especially useful to recite this prayer in any situation in which you may be in conflict with or hold some judgment toward another person. In that case, visualize that person while offering the following blessing: "Jane, Jack, etc., I honor you and I thank you for your presence in my life." Then add the Lovingkindness prayer in the following form:

> *May you be at peace,*
> *May your heart remain open,*
> *May you awaken to the light of your own true nature,*
> *May you be healed,*
> *May you be a source of healing for all beings.*

The Unity Church Prayer of Protection

The light of God surrounds me,
The love of God enfolds me,
The power of God protects me,
The presence of God watches over me,
Wherever I am God is,
And all is well.

(In this prayer, substitute "Higher Power" or "life"
for the word "God," if you wish.)

One client of ours often felt consumed by fear during her first year of recovery. For April, prayer and meditation were enormously helpful to her in finding inner peace.

We recommended that she repeat this prayer several times a day, as she visualized God's presence surrounding, enfolding, protecting, and watching over her. We also suggested that she repeat, anytime that she was feeling panicked or fearful, the prayer's concluding words, "All is well." Doing so helped her shift out of her fear, as she enlisted support from Higher Power to live more safely and fully.

Prayers for Mealtimes

Many addicted individuals have poor eating habits. Some often partake of food in an unconscious and hurried way, while others are addicted to food itself.

Mealtime prayer can sometimes be an effective strategy for breaking an addiction to food, since it is one way to slow down this "speeding gravy train." We recommend prayer at mealtime, however, for anyone in recovery, whether from food addiction or not.

With mindfulness and prayer, eating can become a more enjoyable, even a sacred experience. Flavors, textures, and aromas become enhanced through conscious eating.

It only takes a few seconds to center yourself and offer a prayer at mealtime. If you are dining out at a restaurant, you can use this prayer, choose one of your own, or simply offer a silent thank-you before you dig in. You may even find yourself in the company of others who would welcome the opportunity to join hands and offer a prayer of gratitude along with you.

Here is a universal mealtime prayer that we recommend to our clients:

Thank you for the blessings
of this wonderful food,
food from the good earth,
food for the mind, body, and spirit.
May it nourish us well
and provide the sustenance
needed to live in harmony
with all creation.

It only takes a moment to offer a prayer prior to eating—and since each of us must eat food daily in order to stay alive, there are innumerable opportunities to do so.

By choosing to eat mindfully and with gratitude for the gift of food, we can profoundly change our relationship with food itself. We can reeducate ourselves to relate to food as the living essence of God/Spirit, not just as stuff to be shoved into our mouths and chewed unconsciously. This change in attitude alters our relationship to food on all levels. Even our digestion and the assimilation of the food we eat improves.

Evening Prayer of Gratitude

If the only prayer you say in your whole life
is "Thank You,"
that will suffice.

—Meister Eckhart

So, as you turn out the lights in the evening, simply say "Thank you" to Higher Power for the gifts of life you have received today. If you like, you can specifically name whatever it is that you are grateful for this day.

We've found that when a human being focuses on gratitude, his entire being shines brightly! This gratitude practice can also be done in the form of a "walking meditation," which we describe below.

Bold and Irreverent Prayers

To be effective, prayers don't have to be serious! A little levity can certainly "leaven" the mix. Laughter is healing, so let laughter lighten your prayer life. A lighthearted prayer can be an effective antidote for the guilt and somber self-preoccupation that some individuals in recovery tend to have.

As we've already mentioned, we do encourage you to be creative. Design your own personalized prayers and have fun in the process. It can also be wonderful to sing a prayer aloud—in the car, in the shower, or in some other way as part of your morning ritual.

Dare to be irreverent! When Barry gets out of bed in the morning, the first words out of his mouth are, "Hallelujah! He is Risen!" That is for him a bold affirmation of life, which carries within it a seed-prayer that the day ahead will unfold in a way that is celebratory in every possible manner.

Earth Blessings Prayer

Finally, here is an "earth blessings" prayer that can be spoken in gratitude for the wondrous planet that all of us share.

Sacred Waters of the Earth
> *Flow through my being*
> *Awakening deep rivers within,*
> *Nourishing the garden of my soul,*
> *Caressing me with the mists of Spirit.*

Divine Song of wisdom
> *Unfurl the lotus petals of my heart,*
> *Reveal the nectar of truth,*
> *The sacred center of knowing.*
> *Let my whole being dwell here,*
> *Drinking truth nectar like honeybees*
> *Alighting on purple clover blossoms.*
> *Deep blue, lavender mist, fire orange*
> *Essence of sky flooding my Being.*

May golden pollen of the sun, moon, and stars
> *Cling to the pores of my skin,*
> *Showering my hair with eternal winds,*
> *Awakening the universe within me,*
> *Dancing the mystery of darkness,*
> *Swimming in cosmic light.*

May the rays of the sun anoint my being with flaming warmth;

May the velvet moonlight awaken me to the silence of the sky;

May the pure silver essence of the stars sparkle in my eyes;

May the darkness of night massage the shadows of my being.

On earth as it is in sky
Darkness as it is in light
Woman as it is in man
Fire as it is in water
Thunder as it is in silence
Wind as it is in stillness

Nourishing a Sacred Earth
Living a Sacred Life
Being in a Sacred Universe

Meditations for Healing in Recovery

Waking up this morning, I smile,
Twenty-four brand-new hours are before me.
I vow to live fully in each moment
and to look at all beings with eyes of compassion.

—Thich Nhat Hanh,
Present Moment, Wonderful Moment

The heart of all that we teach about meditation is embodied in the above *gatha,* or sacred verse, by Buddhist teacher Thich Nhat Hanh; namely, focusing on the present moment, cultivating joy and gratitude for every precious day of life, and dedicating one-self to an attitude of compassion toward all sentient beings, including oneself. In our clinical work, we have seen how the development of these attitudes and attributes—present focus, joy, and compassion—contributes mightily to the recovering addict's successful emergence from relative chaos into health and stability.

> **Meditation is an effective and simple tool for stress reduction, and for the cultivation of a quality of awareness that becomes the living soil out of which the aforementioned qualities can naturally grow.**

Many still have misconceptions about what meditation is. Some have an aversion to meditation, believing it to be a strange esoteric discipline that's too complex for an ordinary person to master or too "far out" to be taken seriously.

One former client of ours, a man two months into sobriety who considered himself to be agnostic, balked at our recommendation that he explore meditation as part of his recovery process. He exclaimed that he was "too old to sit cross-legged on a mountain top and chant some strange mumbo-jumbo!"

We assured him that meditation could in fact be as simple as breathing. We suggested that he keep an open mind about meditation's potential value for him in helping to relieve his agitation, sleeplessness, and mild panic attacks, all of which were part of his withdrawal syndrome. When he did try meditation, he was surprised by the positive results that quickly ensued.

As a beginning meditation student in the early eighties, a psychotherapist we know was having great difficulty just sitting still and quieting his overactive mind. Something his teacher said at that time helped him put the practice of meditation into perspective, however, in a way that roused his interest and spurred him on. Now, he often tells his clients the following story, which he likes to call "If you can worry, you can meditate."

> My meditation teacher was a former Broadway theater
> director. She had entered monastic life and was now
> teaching a small group of students about meditation.
> One day, she asked how many of us were having difficulty
> with our meditation practice. Most of us raised our hands.

She then asked how many of us had spent some time that day worrying. Everyone raised his hand. The focus of our worries was the usual grab bag of concerns—fears about health, money, our spouses, being late for class, and so on.

Our teacher then said something to the class that was very powerful: "I want to assure all of you that you are already masters of the art of meditation—for if you can worry, you are already practicing a form of meditation." She went on to say that "worry meditation" is a single-minded focus on fear—fear of what has already happened, of what is happening now, or of what might happen in the future. When we are practicing worry meditation, she explained, everything other than the object of our fear vanishes. Worry meditation is, in essence, a one-pointed focus on some perceived reality or unpleasant outcome.

She then presented each of us with this challenge:

As we were already spending a significant amount of time each day meditating on fear, which was robbing us of peace of mind and depleting our life energy, might we each be willing to redirect that energy toward meditations that would instead be life-giving and life-affirming? The answer that came back from every member of the group was, of course, a resounding "Yes!"

With that insight about meditation firmly in place, its practice in this new, health-enhancing way became much easier for us all.

What are the potential benefits of meditation?

Herbert Benson, M.D., one of mind-body medicine's pioneering researchers and strongest proponents of "spirituality in healing," has provided a wealth of research data on the benefits of meditation and prayer. The focal point of Benson's medical research over many decades has been that meditation elicits a set of physiological responses collectively known as the relaxation response.

Whenever a person is faced with a frightening situation (or even the memory of a threatening situation—for example, a near-miss car accident), the so-called fight or flight response, mediated by the autonomic (involuntary) nervous system, occurs automatically. During the fight or flight response, certain physiological changes occur, whereas the induction of the relaxation response creates their opposite:

Fight or Flight Response	*Relaxation Response*
Metabolism increases	Metabolism decreases
Heart rate increases	Heart rate decreases
Blood pressure increases	Blood pressure decreases
Breathing rate increases	Breathing rate decreases
Muscle tension increases	Muscle tension decreases

Benson's studies indicate that when the physiological shifts described above for the fight or flight response become chronic, they typically lead to irreversible physiologic damage and life-threatening illness.

Addiction itself—ironically, even the *process of recovery* from addiction!—can be intensely stressful. That sometimes virulent stress tends to amplify the health-destructive changes just described as part of "fight or flight." Thus, the recovering addict is particularly at risk for serious illness. In sobriety, he no longer has the option of using alcohol and other drugs to numb pain, avoid fears, and cope with life's inevitable challenges.

Meditation is one simple and effective way of generating the relaxation response for greater health and well-being. Here are some of the benefits of practicing meditation that we have observed in our clinical practices:

• A diminished likelihood of relapse in the recovery process.

- An increased capacity to be consciously present, with an enhanced ability to focus effectively on what is being said and communicated, both verbally and nonverbally.
- A more relaxed rhythm in daily living, including a less hurried attitude and approach to daily tasks.
- A greater sense of inner peace and calmness.
- A diminution of stress, anxiety, and tension.
- Improved sleep.
- Greater self-acceptance, self-esteem, and self-awareness.
- Increased performance and efficiency in daily tasks.
- Increased clarity and capacity to make important decisions.
- Increased freedom from compulsive behaviors and obsessive thoughts.
- Increased joy, appreciation of beauty, and capacity to have fun!

A Bumblebee Teaches the Art of Stress Reduction

When Roger was a college freshman, he joined a yoga class on campus. Although he was curious enough to go to the class and give yoga a try, he was not really interested in anything "spiritual" at the time. At the second class, his teacher, a skilled and devoted instructor, asked the class to lie on their bellies while he talked them through a simple focusing exercise.

While Roger was focusing his attention on his neck, shoulders, back, and so on, breathing relaxation into each part of himself, a large bumblebee landed on him and proceeded to crawl down his T-shirt.

Roger was highly allergic to bees. Realizing what was happening, he began to panic. His teacher, observing this, began to speak in a calming, soothing voice: "Be still, Roger, relax. A large insect has crawled under your shirt and will not harm you." He instructed Roger to relax each part of his neck and back muscles. In doing so, Roger became so relaxed that he nearly fell asleep. Then the instructor went over to Roger and lifted up his shirt. The bee flew away.

Roger was amazed by what had happened and impressed by the power of his own ability to relax. If he could invoke the relaxation response so quickly and easily, moving from a state of panic into a space of deep peace and calm, then this yoga thing had real practical value. It was worth exploring!

There is no right or wrong way to meditate, although, in our experience, some ways have proven to be more effective than others. As with prayer, there is no magic formula to follow.

With each of our clients we endeavor to tailor a style of meditation practice to that client's individual needs. For example, some clients who tend to be very restless may have a hard time sitting still. For them, a more active style of meditation (like the walking meditation described below) is usually best, whereas for others quiet sitting may be optimal.

Here are two examples of meditation/relaxation practices that can be utilized with those who prefer or who are amenable to quiet sitting.

Conscious Breathing

Instruct the client (or friend) to sit in a comfortable position with eyes closed and to bring her awareness to the breath, simply watching the flow of breath in and out, without trying to change the breathing in any way, just observing. Reassure her that there is nothing to accomplish here, no particular right way to do it. Say, "All that is necessary is your willingness to explore and your choice to participate and be available to any benefits that may be here for you."

Remind her that the thinking mind may be very active, so that just focusing on the breath may not be as easy as it sounds: "But that's OK. If your attention drifts, just bring your mind back to the breathing."

Below is a model script for instructing the subject in conscious breathing.

Please note: Your success in assisting the person may ultimately depend upon how well you yourself do the exercise; that is, it is optimal that you establish, through your own conscious breathing, an "energy template" for her to follow.

Exercise (approximately 8 to 10 minutes):

First, find a comfortable, relaxed position, with legs uncrossed and feet flat on the floor.

Acknowledge yourself for being willing, right now, in this moment, to explore something that will be of benefit to your health and well-being. Your choice to participate, to explore is what counts here. There is no specific "something" to accomplish . . . there is no particular right way to do this. Just allow yourself to be available to whatever benefits may come forth.

Now bring your attention to your breathing, noticing the flow of breath in and out, without trying to change your breathing in any way. Just observe the breath. You may find that you become distracted by thoughts generated by the busy mind. That's fine. Whenever this happens, just bring your attention back to the breath and continue.

As you watch the flow of breath, you may notice that you become calmer, more relaxed. As you notice yourself feeling calmer, allow that calmness to spread throughout your body. Let the easy flow of breath "teach" the rest of you how to be easy too. Notice how effortless this all can be. Nothing to accomplish . . . nowhere to go . . . nowhere else to be but right here, right now . . .

just allowing the gentle rhythm of the breath to calm and relax you . . . (longer pause).

And now, take one full, easy breath, letting the breath out with a little sigh, and gently allow your eyes to open, returning fully to the present time and place.

Conscious Breathing with Mantra

In this variation, instruct the client to focus not only on the flow of breath but on a sound, or "mantra." You may want to assist the client in choosing a word or sound that he will resonate with. This can be a neutral word (such as "one"), a word imbued with positive meaning (such as "love" or "peace"), or a traditional Sanskrit word or sound (such as "om" or "hum").

Whatever mantra is chosen, its function is the same: to give the mind a place to rest from its tendency toward incessant chatter.

This exercise is similar to the exercise above, now modified to include the mantra.

Exercise (approximately 8 to 10 minutes)
First, find a comfortable relaxed position, with legs uncrossed and feet flat on the floor.

Acknowledge yourself for being willing, right now, in this moment, to explore something that will be of benefit to your health and well-being. Your choice to participate, to explore is what counts here. There is no specific "something" to accomplish . . . there is no particular "right way" to do this . . . just allow yourself to be available to whatever benefits may come forth.

Now bring your attention to your breathing, noticing the flow of breath in and out, without trying to change your breathing in any way. Just observe the breath. You may find that you become distracted by thoughts generated by the busy mind.

That's fine. Just bring your attention back to the breath and continue.

And now, each time you breathe in, say the word or sound that is your mantra, silently, in your inner awareness, with your inner voice. And each time you breathe out, say that sound again. Just allow your attention to gently focus on the breath and on your chosen word or sound, so that on the in-breath you focus on the flow of your breathing, and on the out-breath, you say your mantra with your inner voice, repeating this process with every breath, with nothing to accomplish. Just allow yourself to follow the flow of breath and hear the sound of the mantra within you.

As you continue following each breath and saying your chosen sound, you may notice that you become calmer, more relaxed. As you notice yourself feeling calmer, allow that calmness to spread throughout your body. Let the easy flow of breath and the sound of your mantra teach the rest of you how to be easy, too. Notice how effortless this all can be.

Nothing to accomplish. . . . nowhere to go . . . nowhere else to be but right here, right now . . . just allowing the gentle rhythm of the breath to calm and relax you, while you say your mantra to yourself (longer pause).

So now, when you're ready, take one full, easy breath, letting the breath out with a little sigh, if you wish, and gently allow your eyes to open, returning fully to the present time and place.

In general, our goal in working with clients in recovery is to open their minds to the wide range of practices that can qualify as meditations, within the broad definition of meditation that we are offering here. Toward that end, we sometimes help our clients find ways to weave meditation seamlessly into the existing structures of their lives. Gardening, fishing, cooking, eating, taking a walk, swimming, running can each become a meditation, when practiced with the particular intention of *consciously focusing on each aspect of what one is doing.*

Walking Meditation

The difference between any everyday walk and a walking meditation is that, in the latter, there is a conscious choice to be mindful of every step as well as details of the surroundings, all the while focusing on natural breathing rhythms. This intention can transform the experience of walking from something ordinary and mechanical into something conscious and sacred.

Here is an example of a walking meditation that we especially like, one that can help the recovering addict cultivate an "attitude of gratitude" as well as develop serenity and focus.

An eight-year-old boy in southern France has come up with a lovely way to affirm life—by linking each breath with an attitude of gratitude. We heard about him and his tribute to thankfulness from the Vietnamese Buddhist monk Thich Nhat Hanh, whom we have already mentioned.

Here's what young Jacques suggests: Put aside whatever you are doing and go for a walk, indoors or out in nature. Move at a very slow pace, and take the time to notice your surroundings. As you take each step consciously, carefully observe the world around you. Pay attention, too, to your breathing in and breathing out that continues as you walk.

Now, here is the fun part: You get to choose your favorite things and say "Yes!" to them.

This can be any object or any living thing (tree, flower, person, animal, etc.) that you happen to notice. It can be the color of a wall, the pattern of clouds in the sky, a shape, a texture, or the play of light on a blade of grass—anything that catches your attention and your fancy.

Just choose something specific that you like, something in your immediate world that you want to say "Yes!" to, right now. Engage it with your attention, and on your next in-breath say, "Yes . . . Yes . . . Yes!" with your inner voice. Then, on the next out-breath, say, "Thank you . . . Thank you . . . Thank you!"

Practice saying these words not just in your mind but with your entire being. Feel the "Yes!" resonate through all the cells of your body, as if every cell were applauding, offering a standing ovation to whatever you have chosen to attend to and love in that moment.

Continue this walking meditation by choosing something different to focus on each time you breathe in and out. There is so much to be grateful for!

By practicing this attitude of gratitude, by loving the world in this focused way, you will come to know your own special place in the world more fully. You will fill yourself with love and abundance as you contribute to the well-being of all.

Young Jacques believes that this easy practice is a way to cultivate peace on earth, one breath at a time. His message is profound—yet the words are simple:

"Oui . . . Oui . . . Oui . . . Merci . . . Merci . . . Merci!"

Let the "Thank you!" flow from your heart like a clear stream of fresh water, as if it were nourishing the land and helping everything to grow according to its own true nature.

Eating Meditation

In this meditation/mindfulness practice, an everyday experience (in this case, eating a piece of fruit) is chosen as a focus of meditation.

Hold an apple in the palms of your hands. Look at this apple, feel the texture of its skin, its weight, its "feel." Notice its aroma. Contemplate its origins, the mother tree that gave birth to this piece of fruit that you're now holding.

Visualize the apple blossoms in the sunshine and the rain. Imagine—actually watch—the petals falling down as the tiny green fruit appears. The sunshine and the rain continue as the tiny apple grows.

Imagine yourself picking this particular fruit that you now hold in your hands. Slowly bring the apple to your mouth and have a bite of it, mindfully . . . in full awareness of the texture and taste of the fruit in your mouth, with all its life-giving juices. Eat the apple slowly and enjoy this gift of life.

Offer thanks to this apple for its life-giving fruit. Offer thanks to its mother-tree and to the earth for this blessing. Now, each time you see an apple, look deeply into it. You can see everything in the universe in one apple.

We conclude the chapter with this verse by Irish poet John O'Donohue. It is a prayer of deep love and compassion that offers encouragement to anyone who may have "fallen off the wagon" of life and who may now be struggling to break free from the bondage of addiction, in all its many dimensions. (Note: The Gaelic word *currach* refers to a small canvas-covered boat used by Irish fishermen.)

Beannacht (Benediction)

On the day when
the weight deadens
on your shoulders
and you stumble,
may the clay dance
to balance you.

And when your eyes
freeze behind
the grey window
and the ghost of loss
gets in to you,
may a flock of colors,
indigo, red, green,
and azure blue
come to awaken in you
a meadow of delight.

When the canvas frays
in the currach *of thought*
and a stain of ocean
blackens beneath you,
may there come across the waters
a path of yellow moonlight
to bring you safely home.

May the nourishment of the earth be yours,
may the clarity of light be yours,
may the fluency of the ocean be yours,
may the protection of the ancestors be yours.

And so may a slow
wind work these words
of love around you,
an invisible cloak
to mind your life.

6

Sacred Storytelling in Recovery

*The stories of our journeys and [those of] others nourish us,
revealing profound psychological and spiritual realities,
illuminating the inevitable difficulties and realizations of all
who journey along with us.*

*Stories show a path, shine a light on our way, teach us
how to see, remind us of the greatest of human possibilities.
We are invited to laugh, to awaken, to join our journey with
[the journeys of] others. Their stories are our stories. They
have the power to touch us, move us, and to inspire us.*

—Christina Feldman and Jack Kornfield,
Stories of the Spirit, Stories of the Heart

We all carry within us myriad healing stories waiting to be told, woven out of the rich tapestries of our life experiences. These stories can provide a map to help us make sense of the past, bring new meaning to the present, and guide us safely into the future as recovering men and women.

Through stories we can reinvent our lives. In this chapter, we share many stories about the fire of addiction and the sacred road to recovery—stories that contain within them potent seeds of transformation.

Gary, a friend of ours who's been in recovery for the last twenty years, tells this story about limitations, drawn from memories of his childhood in rural Oregon.

Invisible Fences

When I was a child growing up on the farm, we had a herd of cows in our pasture. There was an invisible electric wire surrounding the field to prevent them from getting out and straying too far away. By winter, the grass, which had been mostly nibbled away during the warm season, would be fresher and greener outside the cows' fenced-in pasture.

Sometimes we would have power outages and the electric wire fence would be down for a week or two. I used to look at the cows lying down in the depleted pasture, right next to the now deactivated wire. Sometimes, they would just stare at the border, gazing into the lush green fields on the other side but never moving beyond the boundary defined by the nearly invisible wire they had grown accustomed to over the years. I would laugh to myself and wonder why they didn't take one step over to the other side where the grass was sweet and fresh.

Years later, I laugh at myself, recognizing that this was the way I lived my life under the influence of alcohol for so many years. A whole new way of being had always existed for me, yet I stayed imprisoned in my own pasture of alcoholism.

I realize that even with years of sober living, I have sometimes continued to live my life within the confines of the invisible fences I had constructed. In order to live more fully, I've had to find in myself a willingness to risk breaking free of the pain associated with these fences in my mind— and the courage to step out beyond the known, so that I might taste the fresh green territory of my life.

Argue for your limitations and they're yours!

—Richard Bach, *Illusions*

Barry's commentary, which follows, highlights our mutually held perspective on limitation and possibility:

Years ago, I came upon the above seven words and have never forgotten them. By invoking these words at times when I had begun to lose hope, or at least to lose courage, I have reaped the benefits of the good medicine that they contain. These words have sustained me through many a walk across the desert of self-doubt.

The cows in Gary's story certainly argued for their limitations, because they were conditioned from past experience not to even consider moving beyond the confines of their pasture, lest they feel the shock of the invisible wire. The same maxim applies for recovering addicts who have been preconditioned over the years to avoid pain at any cost and to live in a pasture barren of greenness, even though a fresh pasture full of vitality is within reach, growing all around them.

Entering recovery is like finding the Garden of Eden again, tasting and experiencing the newness and richness of a life that may have existed only as some impossible dream during the years of active addiction.

How often have we both said to our clients, "So, here is your choice: Do you want to argue for your limitations or would you rather advocate for your possibilities? If you choose to argue for your possibilities, then I can support you in seeing what those possibilities are. I will assist you in actualizing whatever it is that you truly want, whether or not you believe right now that you are worthy of having it. Let's take this leap of faith together into the land of possibility."

All addictive behavior is rooted in limiting or self-destructive ways of thinking. These limiting patterns of thought are themselves addictions. Sometimes they become so entrenched and habitual that it may be hard for the individual who's thinking this way to see that he has a choice in how he thinks and feels. The loss of awareness that there *is* such a choice is itself a symptom of the addictive process—becoming unconscious of even the possibility of more healthy ways of thinking and being.

One day when I was contemplating these things the following three-line verse announced itself to me.

All that there is
is what we tell ourselves
about all that there is

The essential message in these words is that *life is story.* What we tell ourselves about the way things are, how life is, how other people are, and especially how we are has a potent impact upon how our lives feel, day by day, and upon whom we ultimately become.

As we travel the road to recovery, it is our imaginations—our daring to dream of what can be possible—that lead the way. In order to dream a bigger dream of what may be, we must find a way to transcend old limiting patterns of thinking and seeing.

The active addict often seems locked into behaviors that are patently self-destructive. And frequently, these patterns continue into the recovery process. As therapists, therefore, we must always look past and through those behaviors to the core of creative possibility that lies just beyond them.

> Whatever the "drama" may have been, no matter how tragic it may appear on its surface, no matter how dangerously close to disaster its "story line" may have veered, our job as therapists is to remember—and boldly affirm!—that every client is a work in progress.

There *can* be a redemptive act in this unfolding play of life. But the therapist and his client in recovery must be its playwriters, co-creating a script in which, ultimately, victory can emerge.

Telling healing stories can invoke this redemptive power. Healing stories can be potent maps of what can be. They can transport us from old ways of thinking into new and healthier ways of living and being as conscious, sober men and women.

Jane, a brilliant, successful actress and visionary artist with years of sober living behind her, tells this story:

Facing My Fear

For thirty years I lived a sober, conscious life and have performed confidently on stage as an actress. Then, one day, for no particular reason that I could identify, I began to wake up in the morning feeling afraid.

I felt terribly anxious and uncomfortable. Over the next few months, this fear became terrifying, though I could still find no cause for it. I was beginning to feel paralyzed. To alleviate the fear, I tried journaling, meditation, and prayer, but the fear kept growing more intense.

After about six months of living this way, waking up daily in total fear, I finally made a choice to confront my fear. I am a very visually oriented person, so it didn't surprise me that my fear came in costume. It was very dark in color and wore a hat.

So I lit a candle one morning and spoke directly to my fear. This is what I said:

"Good morning, Fear! I don't know where you came from or why you are hanging around so long. Clearly you aren't going away, so perhaps it is time for us to become friends and get more personally acquainted." I sat down, "shook hands" with my fear, and made a cup of tea for the two of us.

An amazing shift then occurred. The fear began to dissipate, and I could feel myself growing stronger, more energized, and at peace with myself. I could see and feel the fear diminishing. I began to feel a lightness in my heart. I felt free.

I realized that my fear might never go away completely, but I understood that that needn't be a problem. By befriending my fear, by letting it be a "person" with whom I could share conversation over tea, I was able to fully integrate it as part of myself. It no longer had power over me—or, more accurately, I no longer gave my power over to it.

Jane's story is a powerful example of the importance of facing and naming our fears—of befriending the parts of ourselves that may be causing us pain and suffering. We have shared it with dozens of clients in recovery as an example of dancing with life—however it may present itself—rather than trying to do battle with it.

Here's another story about fear. Fred was a client with a pattern of multiple relapses. Fred was just emerging from the chemical deluge of a three-week binge when he began to go through withdrawal while at an AA meeting. He began to cry and shake, terrified by the feelings that were awakening in him.

Two old-timers in AA, Penny and Jack, came and sat with him for several hours. Fred was afraid of going home that night. He knew that he had a large stash of drugs and alcohol there and was unsure of his capacity to keep away from them.

Jack held Fred's hand and said to him: "You have two choices, my friend. One is to put more chemicals into your system. If you do this, you may feel temporary relief; but I guarantee you, your life will get worse. The other choice is to stick it out and stay sober one day at a time. Recovery is not easy, and the journey may be painful, yet I promise you that your life will get much better!"

Fred remained terrified that he could not live without drugs and alcohol, yet that moment became an epiphany for him. He found that he was able to stay sober from that day on.

We frequently use healing stories as part of our dialogue with clients in recovery. We draw upon our own ever-expanding repertoires. We include many found stories that come our way through the media (radio, television, the Internet, books, magazines) and in conversations. Sometimes we make up a story on the spot, one that's relevant to that particular discussion.

Stories can also include themes or lessons drawn from popular movies. We may give a client an assignment to see a movie such as *Don Juan DeMarco* or *Thelma and Louise,* and then discuss her response to particular themes and life issues that the movie touches upon. Some healing stories have proven to be so valuable and instructive that we've included them as part of a packet of materials that we give our clients at the first meeting.

Most important of all, and most relevant to the process of recovery from addiction, is our dedication to helping the client come to an understanding of—and fully claim—his *power to choose,* rather than feeling like a victim. We believe that one of the greatest gifts that sobriety and recovery can offer is this reclaiming of one's freedom of choice, in which one becomes the *author* of his own life story rather than the *subject* of someone else's.

Here's a story about the power of choice that we've often shared with our clients.

A Wise Choice

Once there was a wise old woman who lived in a small village where she was witch, midwife, and healer. The children of the village were puzzled by this woman, by her acknowledged wisdom and the high esteem in which she was held by most of the villagers.

One day several of the children decided to put the old woman to a test. They were certain that no one could be as wise as everyone claimed this old woman, with her ancient wrinkled face, to be. They would try to make a fool of her. One of the children found a baby bird. He cupped it in his hands and whispered to his playmates, "I will ask the old woman if the bird is alive or dead. If she says it is dead, I will open my hands and let it fly away. If she says it is alive, I will crush it in my hands behind my back and she will see that it is dead."

The children went to the old woman's house and they challenged her with their question. The little boy, holding the bird in his hands, asked, "This bird in my hands, is it alive or dead?" The old woman studied the boy's face, looked directly and compassionately into his eyes and replied, "It is in your hands, my son."

Choosing to see life's possibilities rather than viewing one's time on Earth as a life sentence of struggle and misery is a crucial step in the recovery process. To convey this message to our clients, it is helpful to teach them how to be good storytellers themselves, that is, provide good medicine for everyone who hears their good stories!

How can we initiate our clients into the healing art of storytelling? Here's one example of a teaching story that we've shared with clients, one that is easy to remember and retell. By learning it and absorbing some of its possible meanings, our clients get to flex their own storytelling muscles:

This story presents a paradox, yet it affirms the possibility of free will. Just like the Tibetan master's student, it is best for the client to "choose the good" (that is, whatever is truly best for his highest good and for the good of all concerned). At the same time, he must not pretend to know more than he can about what is ultimately true.

The Tibetan Master Speaks

A Tibetan master was asked by his student, "What is the difference between good and evil?" His reply: "Really, there is no difference—but when you have the choice, choose the good!"

In this story, we are reminded that good and evil are relative terms. It may be useful to suspend judgment and stay open to whatever may prove to be the best path, even if it may not be what we originally thought was right based upon our old ways of telling the story. We learn to adopt an attitude of humility in the face of the complexity of human life and behavior.

Recovering addicts often lose touch with their power to be the authors of their own life stories. They more typically feel like victims, telling themselves stories (and believing them!) of discouragement and hopelessness, tales of how life is always stacked against them. Though they still may have a concept of good versus evil, they may nevertheless be locked into their own limited versions of what those words mean.

A characteristic trait of recovering alcoholics and addicts, in particular those in early stages of recovery, is black and white thinking, seeing the world as either all good or all bad. A story like this one can be used to help open up a dialogue with the client about good and evil.

It can also begin to open a chink in the armor of victim consciousness, break through the veil of confused thinking, and help the recovering addict expand the range of possibilities of how she views her life.

Aaron, an AA old-timer, says this: "The longer I stay sober, the more difficult it is for me to think in terms of distinctions of right and wrong. As I continue to grow in sobriety, I find that I rely more fully not so much on my thinking mind, which likes to categorize things into neat tidy boxes, but rather on my gut feelings and my intuition, which naturally lead me to the choices that serve me best."

Like Aaron, all of us have healing stories to tell. These are our sacred stories that can serve us as transformational tools for healing and self-discovery, especially if we learn to value them and share them with one another.

Here's another true story from AA:

> Once upon a time there was a beautiful woman who had been coming to AA for two years, but she could not seem to stay sober. She continued to relapse and found herself sinking into an ever-deepening hole of misery.
>
> The good news for her was that she kept coming to AA meetings and sharing her story with others. One day, after yet another relapse, she stumbled into the AA club room and encountered a wise elder, a man with more than thirty years of sobriety.
>
> As he walked up to her and took her hand, he asked her how she was doing. The woman burst into tears and said, "I am hopeless, totally hopeless."
>
> Looking deeply into her eyes with love and compassion, he said in a soft voice, "That's wonderful news. I am happy for you. Your way hasn't worked. *Perhaps you are ready now to try our way.*"

This simple statement penetrated her old defenses. It got through to her. She stopped drinking and has remained sober ever since.

Lately, there's been a huge revival of interest in the art of storytelling. Storytelling is one of the most ancient and universal healing traditions on earth. The oral tradition as a means of transmitting wisdom, values, history, and teachings of all kinds from generation to generation was in place long before modern culture emerged. The world's great spiritual teachers were all storytellers.

Jesus taught through parables and so did Buddha. The stories of Mohammed perfuse the Koran.

Peggy Beck and Anna Walters acknowledge the power of storytelling in the following excerpt from their book, *The Sacred Ways of Knowledge, Sources of Life:*

> Human memory is a great storehouse which we ordinarily fill with only a fraction of its capacity. The elders knew this and tested and trained the memory along with the other senses, so that history and the traditions of the people could be preserved and passed on. One of the most important of the oral traditions was storytelling.
>
> One can hear a thousand lectures and remember little, yet a story that has relevance to one's life may be remembered for a lifetime. Angeles Arrien, a Basque folklorist and anthropologist, examined current research by Joanne Martin of the Stanford School of Business, who found that "Illustrative stories told within organizations encourage more commitment, generate more belief, and are more remembered than statistical data that proves the same point in a factual way."

Storytelling helps us remember who we are. It can assist us in examining where we came from in our addictions and where we may be heading in recovery.

Stories are tools for making sense and meaning of our life journeys. They provide valuable blueprints and tangible instructions for living fully, for connecting with ourselves and with one another.

Storytelling is an inherent part of twelve-step recovery from addictions and one of the foundations of every AA/NA meeting in the world. In twelve-step meetings, there is an emphasis on "shared experience, strength and hope." Thus, for people in recovery, storytelling is one of the main vehicles used for communicating personal history and transmitting knowledge and wisdom.

In his treatise, *The Uses of Enchantment,* the psychologist/educator Bruno Bettelheim says, "Our greatest need and most difficult achievement is to find meaning in our lives."

Storytelling helps us fill that need to make meaning of our lives. For the recovering addict, whose inner world may have become devoid of meaning during the active stages of addiction, renewed hope can be found as he rediscovers life's meaning through story. A good story is like a living jewel that continues to sparkle, bringing healing and fresh meaning to the individual and his community for years or even lifetimes.

In the material that follows, we'll share some of our own sacred stories and offer questions for you to reflect upon. As you read these stories, we encourage you to let them percolate through you as a kind of reading meditation. As you do so, pay attention to any thoughts and feelings that come forth.

Wild Pansies and the Mystery of Life

It is mid-winter and the wild pansies are blooming profusely in the garden in the front yard of Dancing Tree, my new home in Rappahannock County, Virginia. The landscape is pure winter—no foliage, but clear skies and all the perennial garden plants and flowers long since fallen asleep for their annual winter slumber. Plant life, once new and fresh, once filled with color and joy, has run out of steam, is now frosted, frozen, and transformed by the powerful forces of nature, as it sinks back into the living soils of Creation. Ashes to ashes, dust to dust . . . the sacred cycle of birth, death and rebirth, cycles older than the moon and stars, all part of the mystery of life.

And there, in the midst of winter's naked beauty and lifeless landscape, is a splash of colors, vibrant lemon-yellow and purple blue-violet hues dancing freely and daring the eyes to look closer and say, "My God, there are flowers blooming in that winter garden!" Not just any flowers but wild pansies, Johnny jump-ups, violets.

I have known for years that the wild pansy is the toughest breed of flower. Winter after winter these joyful, tiny blooming clowns do their vibrant dance in the midst of winter's icy grasp. The daffodils may be sending up small green shoots, yet none dare reveal any flower buds yet. Only the wild pansy dares to sing the sacred song of the flower spirits in mid-winter.

These six little plants entered the soil last October and have been blooming regularly throughout the winter— through several winter storms, five inches of snow, two ice storms, zero-degree weather, wind and rain. Several weeks ago, we had two sunny days that melted the ice around their garden home, revealing their tiny clusters of semi-wilted green leaves and dead blossoms, a bit faded yet very much alive.

On the third sunny day, like the resurrection, new blossoms begin to sprout and emerge from what had seemed to be an icy tomb; and soon, there is a living blaze of color on the frozen landscape, as radiant sunshine-yellow and purple passion blossoms boldly bloom in their celebration of life.

Amazing Grace! We all have much to learn from this tough, resilient, and beautiful wild pansy.

The disease process of addiction and the healing journey of recovery mirror these sacred cycles. Addiction initiates a powerful death phase, including the erosion of our bodies and everything we hold to be ultimate in value—our love of self, of others, and of all creation.

Addiction destroys life. Slowly but surely, like the forces of winter acting upon the life of wildflowers once green and alive, addiction erodes body, mind, and spirit until a human being either fades slowly and inexorably into oblivion or wilts into irreversible decay and death.

The devastation wrought by this death phase of addiction is epitomized by this suicide note that Roger wrote at the age of nineteen, while in the midst of despair:

> There is a bleeding ulcer in my mind and I am wondering how I fit in with humankind. My mind is growing crazy and I am bloated with sour misgivings of my life. All I want is to be blotter paper, soaking up drugs and alcohol until I am tuned out, turned off and torn apart, for there is a bleeding ulcer in my mind, eating away at my life, twisting and turning me into another world, a world of oblivion, a world where desperation rules and the only kind of reality is a grim one.
>
> There is a bleeding ulcer in my mind and my lifeline is burning up, leaving a tiny thread of hope, yet this too is frayed as the ulcer bleeds all over my mind. Sometimes the icy north winds are too strong, engulfing my deluded body and mind, ripping through every vein, every cell of me. My roots are a tangled mess. I am tired of clinging, of hanging on to the tundra-like soil of my body.
>
> I want peace. I am tired of fighting, tired of the endless roller-coaster of extremes, tired of the self-hatred. I want peace.

Roger proceeded to drink a bottle of champagne and swallow a handful of barbiturates—but miraculously, he managed to survive that night and the next day, a bit wilted like the wild pansy after the ice storm, yet still alive.

Like the wild pansy, human beings can have a remarkable capacity to bounce back. Happily, Roger proved to be one of those resilient ones. Within a year, he found the fellowship of Alcoholics Anonymous, went through a rehabilitation program, and has been sober and very much alive, blooming and reblooming every year for the past two decades.

Like the wild pansy, each of us must struggle at times with the ever-changing climate of our lives. Sometimes the storms of life are quite harsh and our inner living garden may feel like barren tundra. The surfaces of our lives may lie heavy, frosted, and broken down by the pain, the struggles, and the challenges of daily life, stripping us down to our core essence.

Addicts and alcoholics have often been characterized as weak-willed and fragile. This is far from the truth. Those fortunate enough to weather the storms of their addictions and enter recovery—those who develop deep roots in sobriety, through AA/NA, community, and so on—can transform any weakness into powerful, ever-blooming strength. And these survivors have a healing message for us all.

Like the wild pansy, when his roots are strong and well developed and he is well anchored in the life-giving soils of creation, each person in recovery can learn to bloom and rebloom, growing ever stronger and more vibrant.

By drinking in the gift of the holy now, by soaking up the nutrients of love, community, service, beauty, and joy, the recovering addict, like the wild pansy, can learn to thrive anywhere, whether in the gravel or the cracks between the stones, or in the fertile rich soils of God's creation.

May we all bloom together, spreading brightness and joy wherever this sacred dance of life may lead us.

Questions for Reflection

1. In what ways is this story relevant to your own life?

2. How strong are your roots? Are you receiving enough nutrients in your life, such as community, rest, quiet time?

3. Pertaining to the suicide note, is there some part of your life that needs to die or be put to rest right now? Perhaps an old destructive pattern of behavior?

4. In relation to your own recovery process, what meaning or insight might you draw from the parable of the wild pansy?

Angels Among Us

Barry tells this story:

> This incident radically changed the way I look at the world around me—and at everyone in it.
>
> I was having lunch at a popular café in downtown Washington, D.C., with my friend Mariana. She was planning to leave the next day for her native Argentina, to reunite with her husband and children. This would be our last time together for some while, perhaps forever.
>
> I was already beginning to grieve the loss of our special friendship. I had looked forward with great anticipation to this last time together. What I hadn't counted on, though, was the hustle-bustle of that trendy little sidewalk café on a Saturday afternoon in mid-summer.
>
> The scene was loud and intense: frantic waiters with too many tables to serve, the relentless clatter of plates, customers engaged in loud conversation crammed together around tiny tables that abutted ours, cigarette smoke drifting into our faces, creaking fans whirring at full throttle in the damp heat.
>
> I felt irritated. I could hardly breathe, let alone hear Mariana talk. Not wanting to miss any of her precious words, I stretched across the table toward her. Sensing my frustration at unwittingly having chosen this noisy restau-

rant for our last rendezvous, Mariana galvanized my attention for a moment and then looked at me intently.

Then she did something that altered my sense of reality: She subtly but masterfully redirected my focus away from our private conversation and back toward the chaotic scene around us. She invited me to look away from her for a moment and gaze outward into the crowd.

Making a sweeping gesture with her hand, she said four simple words to me that I shall never forget: "Look," she whispered, "they're all angels!"

I looked. I took a breath. I saw . . . not only with my physical eyes, but through the eyes of my heart. I saw the truth that this wise friend, in her love and compassion for me and for all the others, had wanted to convey. Indeed, they *were* angels! Every one of them—the waiters, the cooks, the other diners (even the smokers!), the passersby—was an angel. I could see their halos!

Nowadays, when I walk down the street, I always remember that moment in the noisy café where I saw angels everywhere. Now I see angels on every block, along every step of my journey.

Questions for Reflection

1. What are some everyday occasions when you might practice this different way of viewing strangers?

2. Who in your life have you most judged as being a devil? How might you see the angel in that person?

3. What might be the benefits to yourself (for example, inner peace, greater happiness, and so on) of seeing the world as a gathering of angels?

The River of Love

Each day, I have a choice: I can swim in the river of love and faith or in the river of fear and doubt.

Sometimes, I slip into the river of fear, trying to control the flow of life, trying to protect myself from the pains and sorrows of the world by erecting false, flimsy walls around my deepest, truest self. While swimming in the river of fear, I often unknowingly commit small daily suicides and a living part of my soul dies. These little deaths—deaths of my deepest hopes, my potential, my sacred dreams—accumulate in the vast realms of my unconscious.

If I continue to choose to swim in the river of fear, I may one day find myself washed up on the shores of my own graveyard, only to see that it is littered with the weathered bones of my unlived dreams, my unused potential, and my unlived life.

Teach me, Gracious Spirit, to be mindful of my fears and to face my fears consciously. Teach me to choose love and faith over fear. Teach me to swim freely in the river of love and faith—to heal, to grow, and to live more fully in the present moment.

Teach me to be mindful of the two clocks operating simultaneously in my life. One clock draws its power from the river of fear, telling me in a harsh, demanding voice that there is never enough time in the day to live, not enough time for love, not enough energy or resources available within the time frame of a given day. This clock communicates poverty time and poverty consciousness. It feeds my desire to rush through life blindly, running from one destination to another. This way of living and being literally robs me of the time of my life.

The other clock draws its power from the river of love and faith. This clock whispers softly into my ear, reassuring me that I am always right on time—that I have more than enough time, more than enough love, energy, and resources to live an abundant, richly rewarding, and balanced life.

Teach me, Gracious Spirit, how to shift gears from poverty speed to God speed, trusting that all is well in the grace of the present moment. Teach me to be mindful of the whole soup kettle of life. Teach me to break through the obstructions that can dam up my life spirit.

Teach me to swim freely in the river of faith and love.

Questions for Reflection

1. In your recovery, are you finding yourself swimming more often in the river of fear or in the river of love?

2. What have you not been making time for in your life? What unlived dreams, hopes, and aspirations have you put aside because of fear?

3. Do you feel that you have enough time in your life to live a fulfilling, balanced life, or are you living in poverty time?

4. Have you been facing your fears directly?

5. Do you feel relaxed and in the flow of your life? What's working well for you? What's flowing naturally, with ease and grace?

Freedom of Expression

At a dinner party I was having a conversation with a friend named Carlie who is a master chef. I was telling him about the experience I had while traveling in Southeast Asia.

I was enjoying a delicious noodle dish in northern Thailand. When I reached the bottom of the bowl, I discovered what appeared to be a tangled web of seaweed. Upon closer scrutiny I saw, nestled in the bottom of the bowl, a dozen shriveled chicken feet. To my friend who was sitting with me at the table I shrieked, "That is so gross!"

After I had told him this story, my friend replied, "The word 'gross' just doesn't exist in my vocabulary." This master chef went on to explain that by not prejudging any food as gross, he gave himself considerable latitude with his creativity in the kitchen. Virtually nothing was off limits to him. In fact, many of his most wonderful, signature meals emerged out of this bold experimentation.

Questions for Reflection

1. What negative judgments do you hold about your feelings or your life in general? How does this limit your freedom?

2. How might your judgments of yourself, others, or certain aspects of your life be inhibiting the expression of your creative life force in sobriety?

3. What is one *never* that you might be willing to upgrade to a *possible?*

What makes the sharing of stories so powerful? Here's a summary of ten characteristics of storytelling that we've found to be the most compelling in our decision to elevate storytelling to the category of prime healing modality. These aspects of storytelling make it particularly suitable as a potent tool for working with clients in recovery.

1. **Attention/listening.** In hearing another's story and having our own stories heard, we build connection and mutual respect.

2. **Presence.** Stories are engaging. When we share them, we come powerfully into the present moment. We are really there—with ourselves, with the storyteller, and with one another!

3. **Love and caring.** We demonstrate, through our willingness to listen, that we care enough about ourselves and others to want to hear their stories.

4. **Universality.** Stories connect us with our deep roots, with our ancestors on earth who have shared stories since time immemorial. Another's story always seems to touch upon themes that remind us of our own life experience.

5. **Directness.** Stories go directly to the heart of the matter. In telling our stories, we become authentic and direct. We tell it like it is!

6. **Simplicity.** Stories are highly efficient tools of communication. They convey a lot, in simple language and often with very few words.

7. **Fun for everyone.** Listening to stories is fun! Both adults and children enjoy them. The inner child is awakened through this natural enjoyment of story.

8. **Depth.** Stories take us deep, because they speak the language of the unconscious. They can often move us profoundly.

9. **Mystery.** Stories are enchanting, compelling, and mysterious in ways that cannot easily be explained in conventional terms. They connect us, too, with the mystery of life.

10. **Hope.** Stories give us hope. They remind us of what is possible. They coach us to keep on keeping on.

Here is a beautiful story that we received over the Internet. This story teaches a lesson of love and support, even when the odds appear to be stacked way against you, that is very pertinent for people in recovery.

That's My Child

I was watching some little kids play soccer. These kids were only five or six years old. They were playing a real game, a serious game—two teams, complete with coaches, uniforms, and parents. I didn't know any of them, so I was able to enjoy the game without the distraction of being anxious about winning or losing. I wished the parents and coaches could have done the same.

The teams were pretty evenly matched. I will just call them Team One and Team Two. Nobody scored in the first period. The kids were hilarious. They were clumsy and terribly inefficient. They fell over their own feet, they stumbled over the ball, they kicked at the ball and missed it, but they didn't seem to care. They were having fun.

In the second quarter, the Team One coach pulled out what must have been his first team and put in the scrubs, except for his best player who now guarded the goal. The game took a dramatic turn. I guess winning is important even when you're five years old, because the Team Two coach left his best players in, and the Team One scrubs were no match for them.

Team Two swarmed around the little guy who was now the Team One goalie. He was an outstanding athlete, but he was no match for three or four who were also very good. Team Two began to score. The Team One goalie gave it everything he had, recklessly throwing his body in front of incoming balls, trying valiantly to stop them. Team Two scored two goals in quick succession. It infuriated the young boy. He became a raging maniac—shouting, running, diving. With all the stamina he could muster, he covered the boy who now had the ball, but that boy kicked it to another boy twenty feet away, and by the time he repositioned himself, it was too late: Team Two scored a third goal.

I soon learned who the goalie's parents were. They were nice, neat-looking people. I could tell that his dad had just come from the office. He still had his suit and tie on. They yelled encouragement to their son. I became totally absorbed, watching the boy on the field and his parents on the sidelines.

After the third goal, the little kid changed. He could see it was no use, he couldn't stop them. He didn't quit, but he became quite desperate. Futility was written all over him. His father changed, too. He had been urging his son to try harder, yelling advice and encouragement. But then he changed. He became anxious. He tried to say that it was okay to hang in there. He grieved for the pain his son was feeling.

After the fourth goal, I knew what was going to happen. I've seen it before. The little boy needed help so badly, and there was no help to be had. He retrieved the ball from the net and handed it to the referee and then he cried. He just stood there while huge tears rolled down both cheeks. He went to his knees and put his fists to his eyes—and he cried the tears of the helpless and brokenhearted.

When the boy went to his knees, I saw the father start onto the field. His wife clutched his arm and said, "Jim, don't. You'll embarrass him." But he tore loose from her and ran onto the field. He wasn't supposed to. The game was still in progress.

Suit, tie, dress shoes, and all, he charged onto the field, and he picked up his son so everybody would know that this was his boy, and he hugged him and held him and cried with him. I've never been so proud of a man in my life. He carried him off the field, and when he got close to the sidelines I heard him say, "Scotty, I'm so proud of you. You were great out there. I want everybody to know that you are my son."

"Daddy," the boy sobbed, "I couldn't stop them. I tried, Daddy, I tried and tried, and they scored on me."

"Scotty, it doesn't matter how many times they scored on you. You're my son and I'm proud of you. I want you to go back out there and finish the game. I know you want to quit, but you can't. And, son, you're going to get scored on again, but it doesn't matter. Go on now."

It made a difference. I could tell it did. When you're all alone and you're getting scored on and you can't stop them, it means a lot to know that it doesn't matter to those who love you. The little guy ran back on to the field and they scored two more times, but it was okay.

I get scored on every day. I try so hard. I recklessly throw my body in every direction. I fume and rage, the tears come, and I go to my knees. And my Father—my Father— rushes right out onto the field, right in front of the whole crowd . . . the whole jeering, laughing world. And He picks me up, and He hugs me, and He says, "Child, I'm so proud of you. You were great out there. I want everybody to know that you are my child."

Creating a Story Circle

Here's a final suggestion: Consider creating a story circle. A story circle is a place for friends, including those in recovery, to meet and share the stories of their lives in a way that can be healing for everyone. It can provide a forum for friends to connect more deeply with one another, for having fun and celebrating life and learning.

For three years, we co-facilitated a storytelling gathering for our community. We met once a month at a friend's home. Our intention was to create a venue for sharing stories drawn from the events of our everyday lives.

At these gatherings, no one was a storytelling expert. These were ordinary stories about ordinary lives. Yet, in the telling of these stories we experienced healing and delight. No one was pressured to speak. No one was required to tell a story, but most everyone did.

We chose a theme, set a time and date, and met in a candlelit setting, which helped set a tone for relaxed intimacy. The range of possible themes is huge, so be creative!

Here are some of the themes that have worked well for us:

- Humor—funny stories in recovery and in life
- Wisdom stories—from AA/NA, stories from wise teachers we've met along the way
- Stories of amazing grace
- Stories about broken relationships and their healing
- Stories of animals and how they have gifted us with their presence
- Stories of love and service
- Stories of how challenges became blessings
- Stories of death and resurrection—how losing loved ones made us more fully alive

After introducing the theme, each of us would say his name and tell a brief story. Then some of the participants would tell longer stories. At the amazing grace meeting, for example, participants shared stories about the variety of ways that grace had unexpectedly appeared in their lives. Some participants were moved to tears, others to laughter. Afterward, everyone went home with a full and happy heart.

People in our community circle still talk about how powerful the story circles were for them. Stories do move us in mysterious ways, and we usually remember a good story for a long time.

We found it helpful for one or two people to serve as facilitators, taking responsibility for choosing and announcing the theme, selecting a time for the meeting, inviting the participants, and preparing sacred space. We've found, too, that familiarity and intimacy are often enhanced by having the story circle meet at a consistent location.

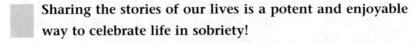 **Sharing the stories of our lives is a potent and enjoyable way to celebrate life in sobriety!**

As we see it, the world is made of stories. In virtually every culture, stories are the building blocks of intimacy, the foundation of human connection. Learn from your stories and share them with one another, in the spirit of love and healing.

7

Healing Rituals for Recovery

The word *ritual* derives from a root word that means "to fit together." It is related etymologically to the words *art, skill, order, weaving,* and *arithmetic,* all of which have something to do with fitting things together and integrating them to create order.

The root word for *healing* is *hale,* or "to make whole." Healing rituals, then, provide us a means of weaving and fitting together different aspects of our life experiences. In the process, we become more healthy, whole, and vibrant.

In the psychological traditions in which we have been trained, ritual often has a negative connotation. In that context, rituals are most often associated with compulsive behaviors that some individuals can become trapped in—so-called ritualistic behaviors, like repetitive hand washing or repeatedly checking and rechecking to be certain that the door is locked or that the oven is turned off.

In our discussion of ritual as a healing modality, we introduce a very different context. Here, we explore ritual as a symbolic, life-affirming action that is consciously and deliberately chosen for the purpose of liberation and personal transformation.

We recommend the use of ritual for recovering addicts as a potent way for them to free themselves from the darkness of past destructive patterns and emerge into the daylight of free choice. In this context, ritual becomes a way of revealing, or making visible, these new and healthier ways that, at some level, have been clamoring to be born.

As innovative health practitioners, one of our intentions has been to introduce clients to the fertile domain of healing ritual. Over the years, we have worked co-creatively with our clients, designing hundreds of healing rituals tailored to each client's needs. In doing so, we have found the use of ritual to be a powerful strategy in our transformational work. Indeed, we have discovered on many occasions that conscious ritual as an approach to healing can often bring extraordinary richness into the therapeutic arena, especially with recovering addicts.

The healing rituals we describe in this chapter can help promote recovery from addiction by providing a context for a deepening sense of well-being and connectedness. Each one is a map, or set of directions, that points toward sober living and encourages awakening. These structured rituals can help individuals participate more fully in the celebration of life's possibilities.

Our goal for this chapter is to elucidate the healing power of conscious ritual in everyday life and to provide instructions for its successful implementation. We've deliberately chosen rituals that have helped our own clients, ones that are readily accessible and easy to understand. First, here's a brief summary of our views on the nature and value of healing rituals in the recovery process:

1. Rituals are specific tools for multidimensional healing, which assist people in becoming more conscious, sober, and fully alive. Through ritual we come to *recognize and consciously*

honor specific aspects of our life journeys. We pause and reflect. We acknowledge and celebrate the sacredness of everyday life.

2. Through ritual we take conscious, specific actions that honor, support, and awaken our *innate healing power.* As we take such actions, in an attitude of love, honesty, and surrender, we connect more fully with a reservoir of power and strength—a Higher Power, as it is typically referred to in AA—by tapping into a divine source of inspiration and healing within ourselves.

3. Healing rituals provide pathways for honoring the beauty and the preciousness of life. Through ritual, we become more *consciously connected* with all aspects of life.

4. Rituals help us make meaning out of the suffering and pain that, for most of us, are an inevitable part of growth. They can be a *healing balm* for our emotional wounds. Rituals can be an antidote to the feelings of isolation, loneliness, and despair that addiction generates, thereby bringing the recovering addict into closer touch with his own genuineness, in community with the vibrant world in which he lives.

Healing rituals can be very simple or extraordinarily complex. They all have in common their potential for transforming individual lives through an expanded awareness of the meaning of life.

In modern Western culture, we've increasingly lost touch with meaningful ritual as part of everyday life. Sacred ritual has been largely replaced by repetitive, mostly unconscious, patterns of living: getting out of bed (often in a mental fog or semistupor), bathing, primping or shaving, eating (typically on the run), driving a car (mostly on automatic)—patterned behaviors with little significance or meaning, except in the most mundane sense.

> **The disappearance of meaningful ritual is a modern cultural tragedy that has left individuals feeling disconnected from the "juiciness" of life and bereft of a certain sense of aliveness.**

In the following commentary, Swiss psychiatrist Dr. Carl Jung touches upon the importance of ritual in human life:

> Where do we live symbolically? Nowhere, except where we participate in the ritual of life. But who among the many are really participating in the ritual of life? Very few. Have you got a corner in your house where you perform the rites as you see in India? Even the simple houses there have at least a curtained corner where the members of the household can lead the symbolic life, where they can make their new vows or meditation. We don't have it; we have no such corner. We have our own rooms, of course—but there is a telephone which can ring at any time and we must always be ready. We have no time, no place. . . .
>
> Only the symbolic life can express the need of the soul—the daily need of the soul, mind you! And because people have no such thing, they can never step out of this mill—this awful, grinding, banal life in which they are "nothing but." . . . These things go pretty deep, and no wonder people get neurotic. Life is too rational; there is no symbolic existence in which I am fulfilling my role, my role as one of the actors in the divine drama of life.

This pointed philosophy presents us with a challenge—to move beyond the spiritual emptiness so prevalent in our modern times. We must reclaim ritual as a bridge to the sacred; indeed, into the very essence of what it means to be sober, conscious, and fully alive.

Here is a selection of specific healing rituals that we have found most useful.

Greeting the Day

Materials needed: A bowl or jar of flour, cornmeal, or birdseed.
Time required: Approximately two to five minutes.
Purpose: Setting a positive tone for the day to unfold gracefully.

The manner in which we awaken and greet each day affects the way we feel throughout the day. This ritual describes a way to set a positive, life-affirming tone. It establishes a vital energetic pathway along which the day can unfold.

Fill a jar or bowl with wheat flour, cornmeal, or birdseed and place it where you will easily find it in the morning. (You may want to choose a special vessel that you reserve for this use.) Let this flour or birdseed represent the food of creation. Let it symbolize the essence of life on planet Earth.

Upon awakening, carry the jar or bowl outdoors. Place a few pinches of this food for life into your cupped hands and offer it for the good of all Creation as you say the following:

Gracious Spirit/God . . . I pray that the path to maximum goodness,
prosperity, beauty, service, and love open within me
and all around me as I walk my life journey today.

Now, blow the food out of your cupped hands onto the ground and proclaim, either aloud or silently to yourself, "Let it be so."

As the flour flows back into the earth, into the soil of creation, your intention is cast forth along with it and planted where it will flourish throughout the entire day.

If you can, perform this ritual consistently for thirty days, taking note of any changes, subtle or otherwise, that occur in your life.

Lighting a Candle

Materials needed: A candle of any shape or size; matches.

Time required: About three minutes.

Purpose: This ritual is a quick, simple way to ground and center
yourself at the beginning of the day. It is also ideally suited
for putting the day to rest before going to sleep.

For most of human existence, candles, lanterns, and open
fireplaces have been primary sources of light. There's nothing in
modern times that can adequately substitute for the special
ambiance that candlelight provides. The warm glow of natural
light is simply unparalleled. Candlelight has a nearly instanta-
neous calming effect on human beings. Yet candles often remain
on tables unlit as little more than decorations.

Colleagues, clients, and friends often comment on how frequently our homes and offices are aglow with lit candles. It's true
that we light candles virtually every day of our lives. (We buy
them inexpensively in bulk.)

We each light a special candle at the beginning of each workday. Roger's daily candle is nestled in a terra-cotta sculpture called
the "circle of love." This sculpture depicts a community of men
and women, standing arm-in-arm and forming a sacred circle, with
the lit candle in the center. Barry's special candle is scented with
the natural essences of spruce, lavender, or nutmeg. It sits atop a
little handmade Shaker table that serves as an altar space.

Prior to lighting our sacred candles, we offer a prayer of intent.

*May the light of God's Spirit be present in this room throughout the
day, bringing light and healing for me and for my clients.*

Then, as our clients come into the office throughout the day,
the lit candle—and the blessing it carries—is always there to welcome them.

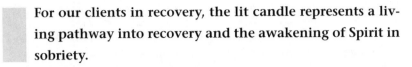

> **For our clients in recovery, the lit candle represents a living pathway into recovery and the awakening of Spirit in sobriety.**

Here's how to perform a candle-lighting ritual yourself. Sit quietly for a moment with the unlit candle in front of you. As you light the candle, recite this prayer, silently or aloud, "May the light of God's Spirit illuminate my path as I walk through this day." Use whatever words say it best for you; that is, "the light of nature, goodness, truth," and so on.

Or alternatively, say, "May the light of sobriety consciousness shine brightly within my being."

Spend a minute or two holding this intention in your awareness while gazing into the flame. Breathe in and out slowly and consciously several times as you anchor your intention deeply into your being. Silently thank the candle for its light. And then, knowing that you will be relighting it again and again, blow it out.

Planting Seeds for New Life, Expansion, and Change

Materials needed: Birdseed or acorns.
Time required: A few minutes or longer.
Purpose: Initiating life changes and transitions.

All changes, even those that are considered to be the most positive, can create stress and activate fears. Perhaps you are embarking on a new career path, getting married or divorced, moving to a new home, interviewing for a new job, or making changes in your health by losing weight or getting more exercise. If so, this ritual can show you a way to consciously sow seeds of change, now and for the future.

For example, Joe, a client of ours, was at a crossroads in his life. He had just completed a two-year consulting job with a pastoral counseling center. It was time to move on. But he was fearful of the change, especially of its potential impact upon his finances.

The consulting position had been a security blanket for him. He wanted to launch a new practice in a rural setting, because he yearned to live in the country. That felt like a risky plan, however. There was certainly no guarantee that he would attract any new clients there.

Nevertheless, Joe decided to resign from his old job and move forward into unknown territory. He immediately formulated some specific goals. His intention was to create a thriving part-time practice in rural Maryland, where he could spend more time in the beautiful countryside that he loved. So he had business cards printed and began to make contacts in the neighboring community.

Meanwhile, we suggested this ritual to him, in support of his cherished goals. We instructed him to go to the farmers' co-op and buy a pound of sunflower seeds. (Joe was fond of sunflowers. He loved their powerful stalks, large seed heads, and the riot of golden petals they produced.) We told him to place the seeds in a special bowl and offer a prayer that those living seeds might seed the new growth that he desired and serve as living symbols for the psychotherapy practice that he wanted.

Over the next few months, wherever he went to make a personal or professional contact, Joe was to take a handful of seeds with him. After each meeting, he was to scatter the seeds on the earth and pray that those seeds would sprout and grow as living symbols of the flourishing of his new practice.

As he performed this seeding ritual during those groundbreaking months, Joe felt a deepening sense of empowerment and gratitude. Within six months, he had surpassed all his goals for the year—and there were a lot of sunflowers blooming in his new neighborhood!

To perform this ritual yourself, buy a small quantity of bird-seed or collect some flowers or acorns. Place them in a special container or bowl. Dedicate these seeds in support of the specific changes that you're making in your life and activate them with this prayer:

> *May the changes I am initiating come to fruition.*
> *May my life and my dreams flourish and prosper.*

These seeds hold the power and promise of new life. Each seed contains the blueprint for a new living plant.

Let the seeds represent the fulfillment of your intentions. Walk outside and cast the seeds onto the earth, asking God and the Universe for your prayers to be heard.

Creating a God Box

Materials needed: A simple cardboard box or large envelope.
Time required: Ten to twenty minutes to create a personalized
God Box (if you choose to personalize your box); several
minutes each day to use it.
Purpose: Creating a daily practice for releasing fears.

We learned this practical ritual during our participation in twelve-step fellowships. Our clients have found it to be a very useful and transformative tool for helping them release their fears.

Fear can occupy a large part of one's inner focus. Creating a God Box is a way of naming our fears by writing them down—in this case, on an index card or scrap of paper. (If you prefer not to use the word "God" or have an aversion to the term "Higher Power," just let the box be your "Healing Box.") When we're able to name something that's been causing us distress, its power in our lives diminishes.

Find an ordinary cardboard box with a lid, or a large envelope, and designate it as your God Box. If you want, you can personalize it by making a collage or painting the outside. That way it can be a beautiful and special part of your living space. If you prefer, it's fine to use the box or envelope undecorated. The key is that *you* know the purpose of this ritual box.

Use this God Box whenever you find yourself preoccupied with fears. Jot down the nature of the fear on an index card or scrap of paper, date it, and simply drop it into the box. (For example, "October 15. Today I am feeling scared about my health. I'm worried that when I go to the doctor next week, she will tell me that I have a serious infection in my lungs that will require me to stay in bed, and I cannot afford to do that. The children need my attention and there is no one else here to take care of them.")

Don't open the box for three months. Each time you place a card in the box, consciously turn your fear over to God, your Higher Power, or the Universe. *It is important not to overthink.* Just practice naming your fears and depositing them regularly into the box or envelope.

At the end of three months, open the box and review what you've written about your fears. Our clients have often been amazed at how few of their fears actually came to fruition. Through this ritual they come to recognize that focusing on fear was often a waste of precious energy that could be used to better purpose elsewhere.

Now, throw away all the cards or slips of paper—and, if you like, begin the process all over again.

Making Your Bed: Creating Order and Balance in Your Life

Materials needed: The bed that you normally sleep in.

Time required: A few minutes.

Purpose: To create more order and balance in your life.

Human beings need order and balance in their living spaces so that they can conduct their affairs more efficiently and feel more peaceful inside. It's good to come home to a bed that is already made. This generally feels more welcoming, as a sanctuary where body and soul can take their rest.

Prior to making your bed, affirm the following: *As I make this bed, I pray that my whole life today may feel balanced and in order.*

As a variation, create a simple ritual to give yourself a special welcome when you lie down in bed at night. For example, one client of ours who loves to read short stories turns down a corner of the sheets as he makes his bed in the morning and places one of his favorite books on his pillow. He tells us that he feels nurtured by this warm welcome that awaits him as soon as he gets into bed at night.

Dedication: Sounding the Bowl

Materials needed: A brass (or glass quartz) singing bowl of any size; two strikers.

Time required: A few minutes.

Purpose: Linking one's life with a broader context and adding emphasis to an intention that one has chosen; clearing the air before a session begins.

One antidote to the feeling of separateness that many of our clients in recovery struggle with is to include this ritual in the session. An action or intention becomes consciously linked with a broader purpose or context while a singing bowl is sounded.

As the session begins, the client is invited to dedicate the meeting to someone important to him, or to some idea or purpose that he cares about. For example, the client may choose to dedicate the session to his father and/or his mother in gratitude for the gift of life given him, or with gratitude for his brother who is undergoing rehabilitation, or in celebration of a teacher who has inspired him, or in support of a political leader who is working for world peace. Or he may dedicate the session to the preciousness and beauty of life, or to the dream that everyone on earth might have enough food to eat, or to the welfare of the astronauts who are orbiting the earth in the space shuttle.

Making a dedication like this is a way of acknowledging and strengthening one's connection with others, and of linking one's own life goals to some broader purpose in which one believes.

After the client has decided to whom or to what the session is to be dedicated, invite him to join you in "sounding the bowl in celebration of . . ." that person or ideal. We have found this to be most effective when both persons strike or activate the bowl simultaneously. (We prefer the wording "invite the bowl to sound" rather than "strike the bowl," because that is more in keeping with the spirit of gentleness and harmony that we wish to cultivate.)

The bowl can either be placed on a table or held in the practitioner's hand while client and therapist invite it to sing. Each person holds a striker while the therapist invites the client to activate the bowl along with her in honor of the person or ideal chosen. Practitioner and client then sound the bowl together.

They refrain from speaking, focusing their attention instead on the object of the dedication and the sound that the singing bowl makes, until the sound becomes inaudible and only silence remains. They maintain this silence for thirty seconds or so before talking, noticing how the air has been cleared for the talk session to begin.

Another way that the singing bowl can be used is for adding emphasis to a choice or intention that the recovering addict has voiced. For example, if the client has stated his intention to remain sober for the rest of his life, the therapist/guide can invite him to sound the bowl in honor of that intention.

Any intention can be amplified in this way. It needn't be a major issue. For example, one client recently invited the bowl to sound in honor of her intention to complete and mail a letter that had been lying on her desk for several weeks.

Ending a Relationship

Materials needed: About three yards of string; scissors; a photograph of the person with whom one has been in a relationship.
Time required: Five to ten minutes.
Purpose: Effecting a clean break in a relationship that has ended or has nearly ended.

It is not uncommon for marriages and other primary relationships to change form or to end once a former addict becomes sober. Sometimes, too, old friendships have to change or die to make room for new and healthier relationships.

It is always stressful to let go of a significant relationship. In our culture we have elaborate ceremonies to honor marriage, yet few, if any, rituals or ceremonies that honor divorce or other endings. This ritual is a simple way to honor such life changes and to help an individual in recovery create a clean break with a past relationship.

Find a photograph of the person from whom you are separating and place it on a table facing you. (If no photograph is available, find something else that can represent that person's presence in your life.) Take a long piece of string and tie one end around your waist or finger. Attach the other end to the photograph. Now, stand in front of the photograph and feel the appreciation you've felt for that person by recalling the gifts you've received as a consequence of being in a relationship with her.

Silently or aloud, affirm that "I honor you for helping me grow, and now it is time for me to move forward in my life. I release you from my life and pray that we may each grow and prosper on our life journeys."

Now, take a pair of scissors and very deliberately cut the cord. Remove the string from your finger or waist and from the attached photograph. Discard it! Be attentive to any feelings that come up as you do so. Then take a little time to rest and reflect upon what you have accomplished.

A Sacred Shower: Cleansing Fears and Negativity

Materials/venue needed: A shower; soap.
Time required: Several minutes.
Purpose: Cleansing fears and doubts from one's mind.

At times we may find that we are preoccupied with fears and doubts—fears about financial security, relationships, challenges to our health. Sometimes we may wake up on the wrong side of the bed and, for no apparent reason, feel disconnected or in a depressed mood. Since most of us take a daily shower, using that shower as a healing ritual may be an efficient way to address our fears and doubts.

Prior to showering, spend a few minutes getting in touch with your doubts and fears. Suspending self-judgment as much as you can, just notice how you feel, letting whatever you feel be OK. What are you most afraid of right now? What might life be like without it?

Now, turn on the shower and adjust the water to a pleasing temperature. As you step into the shower and experience the warm water cascading over your body, offer a prayer of thanks to your Higher Power, either aloud or in your mind's eye:

> *Gracious Spirit, I pray that you may wash away*
> *all my fears, doubts, and worries.*
> *May the sacred waters of this good earth cleanse*
> *my body, mind, and soul.*

Feel the warmth of the water comforting you as you lather your body with soap. Focus upon your current fears, one at a time. Feel them washing away and flowing down the drain as you willingly release them back into the earth. When you're finished with your shower, say a prayer of gratitude for your life, in whatever way you wish.

Watering Flowers and House Plants

Materials/venue needed: A house plant or outdoor garden.
Time required: Thirty seconds to several minutes.
Purpose: Feeding and nourishing your dreams, wishes, and choices.

Most of us have plants in our house or garden that require regular watering to sustain their health and promote new growth. Our dreams, hopes, and desires also require nourishing if we are to grow and thrive as human beings.

Select a house plant or an outdoor garden plant to use in this ritual. Prior to watering it, hold the following intention in your awareness:

As I water this plant, I choose to enjoy watering all of creation
and to be honoring the greening power inherent in life.
I pray that my life, my dreams, and my hopes may remain
fertile and moist—and grow, grow, grow!
Make it so.

Cleaning Eyeglasses/Contact Lenses

Materials needed: Soap; water; a paper towel or contact solution.
Time required: Several minutes.
Purpose: Clearing away self-limiting thoughts, fears, or anxiety.

People who wear eyeglasses or contact lenses generally have to clean them daily to maintain proper vision. Years ago, Roger (who wears eyeglasses) was meeting with the director of an organization for which he worked. He had come to tender his resignation. He had had many conflicts with this new director, and his heartfelt intention on that occasion was to maintain his cool and speak clearly and honestly.

Feeling apprehensive about the meeting, he took a few moments to use the men's room. While he was there, he noticed that the lenses of his glasses were filthy, so he took them off to wash them in the sink.

He then paused and said the following prayer to anchor his intention more fully:

Gracious Spirit, as I wash these glasses, I pray that any dirt or debris
that obstructs or clouds my path to clear vision be removed from my
consciousness, so that I may see and act clearly and lovingly.

Roger washed and dried his glasses, holding the intention that he might see clearly on all levels. He then went to the meeting feeling refreshed and grounded—and easily completed his mission.

This simple ritual can be used as a daily practice for consciously clearing internal debris that may be clouding one's vision. Reflect upon the nature of the conflict or block that you're experiencing and utilize the prayer above or one of your own, holding that intention in your awareness as you're cleaning your glasses or contact lenses.

If you don't wear corrective lenses, hand washing may be used instead. As the client washes her hands, she can say the following:

Gracious Spirit, as I wash my hands, I pray that any dirt or debris that obstructs my path to clear vision and effective action be washed from my consciousness so that I may see and act clearly and lovingly.

Breaking Free of Dead-End Patterns and Behaviors

Materials/venue needed: A dead-end road or path; a journal or note pad.

Time required: Fifteen to thirty minutes.

Purpose: Breaking free of dead-end patterns that no longer serve us.

This is a healing ritual we have used with clients in recovery who may feel at the end of their rope because of particular destructive patterns in their lives. This ritual can be a powerful way of symbolically owning or feeling the weight of a destructive pattern and then immediately moving beyond it, setting the stage for concrete changes in behavior.

We first designed this ritual for a young man who was already three years sober in AA at the time. He had decided to return to therapy, because he found himself continuing a pattern of destructive, abusive relationships that always left him feeling depleted and depressed. He was also nearing the end of his career as a salesperson and realized that he was ready to make a shift into work that would have greater meaning for him.

Additionally, he was feeling that it was finally time to move away from the small town where he had lived all his life and in which he now found himself stagnating. He dreamed of moving to the Northwest, perhaps to Portland. Dead ends had clearly become a prominent theme in Raymond's life at this juncture.

We began by asking Raymond to reflect upon each dead-end relationship that punctuated his life, and to recall the work he'd been doing in therapy in support of changing those patterns. We encouraged him to write down his thoughts, feelings, and insights in his journal. We then planned a session with him that would be "on location."

We took Raymond to a dead-end gravel road near our rural office. Upon arrival, we asked him to close his eyes and to literally *feel,* one at a time, the weight of each dead-end relationship in his life on his shoulders, his emotions, and his spirit.

In recalling these dead-end patterns, we asked him to include not only his personal relationships but also those dead ends that pertained to his job and his living environment. We then asked him to hold this energy consciously as he walked very slowly for about ten minutes along the dead-end road. As he neared the end of the road, we asked him to close his eyes but to continue walking, while one of us took his arm and guided him gently forward.

At the road's actual dead end was a chain (we had chosen this particular road in part because of this feature). Just beyond it was a fresh, grassy path leading into the woods.

When Raymond arrived at the dead end and was standing in front of the chain, we asked him to pause and, with his eyes still closed, to once again feel the weight of all this blocked, stagnant energy that had been weighing down his life and obstructing him in the realization of his goals. We then invited him to let go of all that was old, to open his eyes and behold the new path now looming in front of him—uncharted virgin land.

Raymond then stated his intent out loud, asking Higher Power to help him co-create "a healthy relationship with a soul mate with whom I can share my life journey and have a family." He asked Spirit to grant him the courage to move forward in his life so that he might find the strength to resign from his old job and pursue his dream of moving to the Northwest, where he could engage his passion for art and design.

We then asked Raymond to step slowly and mindfully over the chain while declaring his deep-rooted intention to leave behind the old dead-end patterns to which he had been clinging. He did so, and he emerged onto the fresh grassy path.

At that moment, Raymond felt a profound sense of release and he began to sob deeply. He told us later that, at that moment, he had experienced "this powerful shift in my body."

Within six months, Raymond had completed his move to the West Coast, had entered graduate school in design, and was in the process of creating the life of his dreams. Although he had not yet found his soul mate, he was focusing more of his energy on building healthy, strong friendships in his new location. He had entered what for him was a new world!

Again and again, he had returned in his thoughts to that experience along the dead-end road as he continued to make positive changes in creating a new life for himself.

8

Honoring Beauty— Cultivating the Sacred in Everyday Life

As I walk, the universe is walking with me.

In beauty it walks before me
In beauty it walks behind me
In beauty it walks below me
In beauty it walks above me

Beauty is on every side.
As I walk, I walk with beauty.

—traditional Navajo prayer

In this chapter, we explore the role that beauty and sacred order play in the recovery process. To what extent does the nature of the living environment in which the recovering addict conducts his daily life affect his health and facilitate his successful recovery from addiction?

Not surprisingly, perhaps, we find that many recovering addicts are inattentive to, or seemingly uninterested in, the quality of their living environments. They often tend to neglect their personal hygiene, as well. For example, we've observed a high prevalence of tooth and gum disease among our clients in recovery, who often postpone routine dental care until they are several years into sobriety.

We want to emphasize that by environment we are not just talking about the usual physical factors such as clean air and good sanitation. More pertinent to this discussion are the more subtle influences on well-being—in particular, the entire aesthetic realm. For example, the presence of certain colors, sounds, lighting, and inspiring artwork, as well as plants and other living beings can all affect the health and well-being of an individual who lives and/or works there, and thus his successful recovery.

We believe that beauty plays a significant part in recovery—especially the particular aspect of beauty that we have come to call sacred order. Therefore, we encourage attention to the many aspects of beauty in one's home and workplace as a genuine part of healing in recovery, one that's definitely worth addressing. We view the practice of tending to one's environment, lovingly and mindfully, as a legitimate healing art and a potent factor in the recovery process.

We resonate with the premise that all addiction represents an unconscious desire to connect with Spirit/God/The Sacred through the use of a substance (a chemical, food, activity, etc.) that in reality can offer no more than a transient, substitute kind of pleasure in place of the real thing. Given this perspective, our intention as health practitioners is to help individuals in recovery find something genuinely sacred (and nonchemical) with which to nourish their souls.

We seek to help them discover that in everyday, sober living there are innumerable ways to connect pleasurably with Spirit; in particular, by engaging the realm of beauty and sacred order. Thus, our charge is to help the recovering addict cultivate a taste not only for "clean living" but for the kind of *refined* living that can help her heal her wounds and move along into sobriety.

Beauty and sacred order feed our consciousness. Their presence in our lives awakens in us a greater sensitivity to, and appreciation for, life itself. The practice of infusing the environment in which we live with beauty, as well as noticing and actively appreciating the beauty that's already there, is supremely health-enhancing for the individual and for the society of which she is a part.

> **Beauty and sacred order are by no means casual commodities. They are precious aspects of life, which have the potential to transform our lives by awakening our most subtle sensitivities.**

The Russian artist-mystic Nicholas Roerich expressed his reverence for beauty's power to transform when he said nearly seventy years ago, "The light of art will influence numerous hearts with a new love. We should not only have museums, theaters, universities, public libraries, railway stations and hospitals but even prisons decorated and beautified. This formula which now belongs to the museum and the stage must enter everyday life. The sign of beauty will open all the sacred gates."

By making room for the sacred, by caring enough to make our lives not only functional but holistically beautiful as well, we up the ante in the game of life. We expand the possibilities of what life in recovery—as a fully alive human being—can be.

Feng Shui

We now turn to the ancient Chinese practice of feng shui for some guidelines in the art of creating sacred order and beauty.

This time-tested approach to enhancing vitality has been under-going a modern renaissance as we continue to gain a greater appreciation for the power of beauty/sacred order in promoting health and wellness.

Feng shui (which literally means "wind and water") teaches that every aspect of the world around us is alive. The walls of our homes, for example, are not just material stuff. They are living structures, which in a very real sense are living, breathing organisms, just as we are.

Feng shui affirms that our health and well-being inside is profoundly interrelated with the health and well-being of the world outside us, especially our most immediate environments: our homes and the places where we work.

To be most effective in assisting individuals in recovery, we must view their lives in an *expanded* way that includes their interaction with the environment, or setting, in which they live and work.

We believe that the environment has been a neglected component of virtually all addiction treatment programs. In our experience, facilities that deal with addiction and recovery rarely acknowledge the impact upon the recovering addict of her immediate living/work environment, nor has this been addressed in any practical way in the design of treatment centers themselves as a living context for healing.

In feng shui, however, one's health and the arrangement of objects in the environment are seen as very much interrelated. Feng shui emphasizes and highlights the healing potential of beauty, not only for its aesthetic quality but also for the more significant role it plays as part of a winning strategy for optimal health. In feng shui, the condition of the environment is viewed as an integral part of healing.

> **Feng shui is a traditional health practice that is forever reminding us that when our outer environment is in balance, our inner world is more likely to be in balance, too.**

Restructuring one's living space, indoors or out, can provide a huge change in one's experience and outlook. Consequently, individuals in recovery often benefit from redesigning their environments using feng shui principles—a potent exercise that can help them achieve greater harmony and balance.

One example of this was given to us by Alice, a client of ours who redesigned a corner of her backyard in honor of the memory of her mother. By doing so, she also supported herself in moving more consciously through her grief.

Alice, who had attended CODA (Co-Dependents Anonymous) for many years, had been deeply shaken by the death of her mother, Iris, who had always been a significant figure in her life.

Because Alice had always wanted to do something to beautify her backyard, she chose the occasion of her mother's death to create something that would reflect her own love for her mother as well as her mother's love for the beauty of the natural world.

In a corner of her yard, Alice transplanted a variety of native ferns around the base of an old oak tree. She also placed a birdbath there and filled it with fresh water. Then she engraved a favorite saying of her mother's on a plaque and tucked it into a clearly visible place among the ferns. She placed a little bench there, too, one that was sturdy and comfortable for sitting.

By taking these actions in honor of her mother's life as well as her own love of nature, Alice transformed an unused part of her yard into a living memorial garden filled with beauty and grace. It was now a kind of holy ground for her, a living sanctuary where she could connect with her mother's spirit whenever she chose.

Following are some specific feng shui suggestions to help you and your client get started in creating a health-affirming living/working environment.

First and foremost, remove the clutter.

If there's been a long-standing pattern of disorganization, with unsorted items piled high, this may at first seem too daunting a task. But, by starting small (for example, by focusing on one particular room or surface), you may find that your uncluttering initiative gains momentum and begins to flow more easily.

One helpful strategy is to dedicate yourself to the practice of removing a few unnecessary items from your living/work space each day. This may include items in closets, drawers, or cabinets that are no longer either useful or pleasing to you. Make a commitment to live only with what you love!

Surround yourself only with those things that you've actively chosen either for their practical value or for the ways they bring you pleasure. The biggest challenge may be confronting your unwillingness to let go of items that may be out of date and no longer serving your best interests. For example, that oil painting hanging on the wall over the living room couch that you paid too much for twenty years ago . . . it may be time to bite the bullet: donate it, or give it away, if it no longer represents who you are— or want to be.

Everything in your environment is a mirror, a kind of environmental affirmation, reflecting back to you how you're doing and what you're expressing. In order to feel peaceful and balanced within, you may want to arrange your outer world in a way that resonates with your current choices or heart's desire.

Start with small steps, like the ones we've suggested. Declutter. Get up to date with items you truly want and choose. And acknowledge yourself along the way for your willingness to be a pioneer of inner space as you make healthy choices regarding the world around you—which is nothing less than rehabilitating *yourself* through your own reflection!

Feng shui offers an invitation to anyone in recovery to take a more active role in creating health and well-being by being more actively attentive to his surroundings. If you wish to explore this subject in more detail, please refer to the "Spirituality" section in the Resources for a list of books we recommend.

> *'Tis a gift to be simple, 'tis a gift to be free*
> *'Tis the gift to come round where we ought to be*
> *And when we find ourselves in the place just right*
> *It will be in the valley of love and delight.*
>
> *When true simplicity is gained*
> *To bow and to bend we will not be ashamed.*
> *To turn, turn, will be our delight*
> *Till by turning, turning we come round right.*
>
> —Shaker song

A client of ours learned the impact of beauty and sacred order in his life as part of his recovery process. Here is part of his story.

Jasper was a man so comfortable responding to crisis that he found it difficult just to be. His outer-driven focus, so typical of those in the addiction/recovery process, had essentially ruled him. He made it clear to us, however, that he did want to learn to be more inner-directed. Jasper recognized that his task-oriented, outer-driven way of thinking and being was addictive in nature. He wanted to break free of it.

We reviewed with him some of the ways in which he was already connecting well with his inner self. He told us that he always felt most connected while walking, listening to inspiring music, and doing contemplative reading. In particular, he considered visual beauty an essential way in for him, "like delicious, nourishing food is to a hungry man."

Since he rarely made room for any of these activities in his daily life, our work with him revolved around helping him anchor a heartfelt choice to more fully engage his love of beauty as a way of connecting with his authentic self.

Being an amateur photographer, Jasper was well attuned to beauty and had a well-developed aesthetic eye. Yet this attentiveness to the world at large had not carried over into his personal home and work space. He had made his office into a utilitarian sort of place, totally lacking in aesthetic touches.

We encouraged Jasper to experiment by bringing a special candle and some fresh-cut flowers to his office. When he did so, he found that it made a huge difference in his experience of contentment while working there. He really felt welcomed!

We suggested, too, that he bring in some of his own artwork and hang it on the wall—and that he take a five-minute gratitude walk each day, taking particular note of any appreciation he might be feeling for the beauty he witnessed.

On the home front, we encouraged him to light a candle at dinnertime and to enjoy his meal in quiet without turning on the television. The combination of these simple actions had a major impact on Jasper's sense of inner peace and well-being. In his own words,

> I feel more alive, happier, and I enjoy my days in the office more fully. I realize that I had been "settling for" merely "existing" rather than thriving. When I walk into what used to be a drab office, I now see colorful flowers. I light a candle at the beginning of my workday and I feel so much more energized and alive. Instead of blank walls, I now see my photographs of nature. These have a profoundly calming effect on me whenever I connect with these images.

> At home, when I light a candle now before my dinner
> meal, I feel a much greater sense of peace. This gives me a
> feeling in my own home of sanctuary space.

Another client, an award-winning landscape architect who
had been sober for ten years at the time, was at a point in his life
when he truly wanted a life-mate. Aware that we were likely to
make some equation between characteristics of his living space and
his potential for success in romantic relationships, he requested
that we conduct a session at his home so that we could assess
matters more clearly and make some recommendations.

Jeff had worked hard to bring order and beauty into the entire
upstairs of his home, and for the most part he had been successful. The downstairs, however, was a different story! The guest bedroom was filled floor-to-ceiling with boxes. It was unusable except
as storage space. His own bedroom was dark, cluttered, and
uninviting.

We commented that there appeared to be little or no place
here for a woman to be. There was hardly any room to receive himself! As he thought this over, Jeff began to have more insight about
how the cluttered chaos in both bedrooms was at odds with his
desire to receive and welcome a mate into his life.

He later told us:

> I realize that the state of disarray in my bedroom is a
> reflection of my own fears about intimacy, of wanting a
> mate but at the same time being afraid to have one. No
> one ever touches this area of my house. It has been
> "off limits," walled-off just like me!

To help remedy this situation, Jeff (who is very handy with
tools and construction materials) decided to tear down the wall
between the bedrooms to let in more light and create more of a
feeling of openness. Before embarking upon the actual mechanics

of this project, he wrote down—in *crayon,* on the walls!—his vision for a home that would be welcoming to himself as well as to a potential mate.

As he prepared this foundation of intent, Jeff reminded himself how in the past he had built "rigid walls inside himself" that had blocked him from manifesting what he truly wanted. He determined not to do so again.

He further commented:

> I have been the gatekeeper and more often than not the gate has been tightly shut rather than opened wide. By making a choice to bring beauty, light, openness and creativity into my bedroom, by tearing down the walls (literally!), I am making a choice now to move into the richness that I am capable of, as I make room for the love I already have in my heart.

Bringing beauty and sacred order into his downstairs bedroom area has brought a welcome change into Jeff's life. It's as if a fresh wind has blown through, setting him free inside. He told us that he felt ready now to embody the full meaning of this beloved line from a poem by Rumi: *Let the beauty we love be fully what we dare.*

Examine the fabric of your life. Dare to experiment with bringing beauty and order into parts of your life that have been in disarray.

Beauty can be seen and appreciated even under the most horrendous circumstances. Psychiatrist Robert J. Lifton has written about survivors of the atomic bomb blast in Hiroshima. He tells the story of one man who began weeping uncontrollably at the sight of a single blade of green grass, the only sign of life's persistent beauty amid the hellish desolation that surrounded him.

When we lose touch with the genuine sources of meaning and beauty in our lives, we may end up settling for the watered-down, hyped-up version of beauty that the mass culture embraces. It becomes all too easy, then, to get lost in its cynicism, negativity, and ugliness.

If we think of relapse as a *lapse in consciousness,* it's easy to see how attention to beauty and the awakening consciousness that attends it might diminish that risk of relapse.

> **The more compellingly delightful the environment around and within us, the more likely we are to want to stay connected to that environment and to fully engage it with our eager attention. Then we are more likely to remain sober—so as not to miss the sacred delights so abundantly available in sobriety.**

Abusing alcohol and other substances can numb our bodies, minds, and spirits, but a life enjoyed in the light of conscious sobriety—and attentive to life's sublime beauty—can be a journey of almost indescribable magnificence.

The opposite of *aesthetic* is *anesthetic.* Unless we actively invite beauty into our lives, we run the risk of living anesthetized lives, settling for mere crumbs when life's full banquet table is always set, offering itself to us in every moment.

Actions taken in support of beauty can be simple, like placing a single candle or a vase of fresh flowers on the table as a focal point for an otherwise sterile meeting room, or tucking a small bag full of photos and other small objects having personal meaning into one's suitcase while traveling.

The latter has been a regular practice of ours for many years. When either one of us spends an overnight on the road, he always creates a sacred altar of beloved objects. This can easily be accomplished by arranging these objects on a dresser or night-stand. In that simple way, a nondescript hotel room can transform itself almost instantly into a personal sanctuary imbued with love and good vibrations.

When we facilitate retreats, we often find that the accommodations are bare bones, offering little more than a bed, a writing desk, and a chair. Although this austere simplicity may be appropriate for some occasions of personal reflection, we generally encourage participants to energize their rooms by creating a sacred altar for themselves.

We suggest that they collect items that can be easily found in the retreat center environs (leaves, stones, flowers, etc.) and then arrange these items in any way that pleases them. They are encouraged to include, as well, photographs from their wallets, a ring or some other piece of jewelry, an object of religious significance, or anything else that can help them personalize and beautify their living space.

> **The sacred altar becomes a touchstone during the retreat, a tangible reminder of what truly has meaning. It is something you can visit and become attuned to as you engage in the sometimes arduous process of self-exploration.**

Never underestimate the impact of beauty and sacred order. One personal caveat is that our office bathrooms often draw comment from our clients, who frequently tell us that they want to linger to enjoy the whimsical altars, beauty, and artwork that exist in what is usually a rather stale, utilitarian room. This reflects our desire to have every corner of the house feel like a sanctuary—peaceful, beautiful, and inspirational.

9

A Healthy Immune System in Recovery

Individuals in recovery are recovering from more than just an addiction to a specific substance or substances. They are typically in recovery from an entire way of life that has featured personal neglect on all levels—physical, mental/emotional, and spiritual.

Their immune systems have often been compromised by a variety of assaults and stressors. These typically include, among others, poor eating habits (resulting in deficiencies of essential nutrients and an overload of toxins), lack of adequate exercise, sleep deprivation, poor personal hygiene, strained interpersonal relationships, and the use of caffeine and other chemical stimulants. Thus, any strategy that aims to restore the recovering addict to health and wholeness must include interventions aimed at strengthening the immune system.

This chapter includes a variety of suggestions for doing just that, ranging from cognitive strategies to gentle exercise to the use of mental imagery and focusing techniques. Although it is written as if it were addressed solely to the person in recovery, this material is intended as a resource for anyone working with individuals in recovery, whether as counselor, sponsor, or mentor or more informally as friend, relative, or co-worker.

In our own work with clients of all kinds, we have seen time and time again that specific strategies for change become effective only when the client becomes *receptive* to them. That is, if our client is ever to create an inner garden of healing, the soil itself must first be tilled and adequately prepared.

Consequently, the foundation for healing and successful recovery is rooted in the client's *attitude*. The client must somehow find a secure foothold within his own psyche, a *place of deciding*. She must determine, in some definitive way, that getting well is more desirable than remaining ill, that the benefits of sobriety outweigh those of continuing her old addictive patterns.

On the surface, this would appear to be an obvious and easy choice to make. But our experience has shown us otherwise. The client may have all kinds of compelling reasons, both conscious and unconscious, *not* to change, to be invested in things remaining just as they are.

Therefore, an essential part of our work involves assisting the client in finding and creating an inner alignment with a place of *wanting* to change and of *choosing* to do so. The force of habit, especially an addictive habit, has typically become so strong that overcoming it requires the individual to find some way to align herself with an intention that is even stronger than the dysfunctional pull of the old habitual behavior. Our primary task at that early point in the therapeutic relationship is to help the client become *inspired*—inspired to be free of the drag of what has been, and ready to go for what can be!

As we turn our attention now to the specifics of how to strengthen the immune system, we want to underscore what has just been said: The foundation for strengthening the immune system lies in the recovering addict's making a deliberate, conscious choice for health. This begins with an inner alignment with the intention to have the immune system be functioning optimally. This then becomes part of the more inclusive and far-reaching choice to be healthy.

This is mind-body medicine in action! Setting an intention to be healthy and to have an optimally functioning immune system, by focusing the mind on a choice to be healthy, is a powerful first step in the recovery process. By making this choice, consciously and deliberately, the client comes to an agreement with herself that she is indeed willing to be well, and that, furthermore, she intends to be well and to make choices that are consistent with that positive intention.

Making a choice is like setting one's course, in much the same way that a sailor decides where he ultimately wants to land by deciding what direction to orient the boat prior to pulling away from the dock.

Moving in the direction of what you want—for example, improving the efficiency of your immune system—also requires a candid assessment of where you currently are. In order to do that right now, ask yourself these questions and answer them briefly.

- How am I feeling right now? Am I relaxed or tense?
- Am I feeling easy with myself or rushed, pressured, and on edge?
- How does my body feel? Are there any areas that feel tight or constricted?
- How is my mood? Optimistic and upbeat or pessimistic and discouraged?
- How is my energy level?
- How is my spirit?

Perform this simple assessment in the manner of a reporter who is simply gathering the news, without any particular emotional response (as the detective Sergeant Friday used to say on the old TV show *Dragnet*, "Just the facts, ma'am. Just the facts").

Another part of present reality worth noticing is that today you have chosen to read this book and to do this exercise. You have made it important enough to put other things aside for now and to make your health and well-being a priority. That in itself is a significant step toward better health. Pausing to acknowledge this small step that you are already taking is an important part of building a success track for optimal recovery.

Scientists used to believe that a person's different levels of organization—body, mind, and emotions—operated independently and that conscious intention had little to do with the body's capacity to fend off illness. In that old way of thinking, embraced even by the experts of the day, disease was viewed as something that just *happened* to us.

Current research demonstrates otherwise. Now we know that whatever takes place in one part of us affects all our other parts. We are in fact *energy beings,* existing at different vibratory levels simultaneously.

> **These different dimensions of our humanness, to which we have given names such as mind, body, and emotions, have turned out not to be separate parts at all. They are all interdependent aspects of one whole being.**

In the past decade or two, a new field of investigation has been born, called psycho-neuro-immuno-endocrinology, or PNIE for short. What we are learning—and this has been shown to be true, over and over again, in thousands of studies—is that our thoughts, beliefs, and attitudes have a direct, powerful impact on the functioning of our immune systems.

Through our attitudes and our beliefs, we continually send messages throughout the body/mind/spirit, messages that tell the molecules and cells of our immune systems how to behave. We are *telling* our immune systems what to do, moment to moment, by our attitudes and by our choice of where we place our attention. And our immune systems are listening very attentively!

Alcoholics Anonymous and modern medical treatment programs make this very important distinction regarding personal responsibility: They emphasize that an alcoholic is not *responsible* for having the disease of alcoholism. However, once the alcoholic acknowledges and accepts the reality of her addiction, she does become responsible—in a much more empowered sense—for her recovery.

As we explore the challenge/opportunity of cultivating a healthy immune system during the recovery process, we will certainly want to keep in mind the far-reaching and multidimensional impact that any intervention may have, and the desirability of using a multifaceted approach. In the suggestions that follow, you'll have an opportunity to use the new knowledge that PNIE has brought to light. These simple strategies are offered in the spirit of successful recovery from addiction on all levels and of enhancing the quality of life in general.

Choosing Health

The best way to predict the future is to create it.

—Peter Drucker

As we've already noted, the foundational step in any strategy for immune enhancement is making a deliberate, conscious choice about how you want your health—and your immune system—to be.

> **The key point is this: Your immune system functions according to specific input that you give it about what you want. You are in charge of giving it direction!**

Right now, formulate a choice. Select a few words that describe how you want your immune system to be performing and write them down as a complete sentence. Here's an example: "I choose to enjoy having a strong, optimally functioning immune system that maintains my health magnificently."

Notice that the choice begins with the words "I choose to enjoy." This wording is important. The words "I choose" are a clear and powerful communication to the creative function of your body/mind/spirit. By saying "I choose" you are putting all parts of yourself on notice that, yes, you *intend* to be healthy, and that you are now aligning with that intention. By including the word "enjoy" in your choice, you become a joyful creator, integrating both left and right sides of the brain with the limbic brain.

If you're wondering whether simply writing down a choice about how you want your health to be can have any real impact, we want to assure you that this first step can be a very potent one, which will support everything else that you may choose to do.

Now, go ahead and do it! Decide how you want your immune system to be and write that in your own words into a choice that begins with the words "I choose to enjoy."

An Energy Exercise from Eastern Medicine

According to the Eastern perspective on health, our vitality is directly related to the flow of energy throughout our being. When that energy is flowing well, that is, when it is moving in a balanced, harmonious way, we feel alive and well. When it is blocked, sluggish, or out of balance, we typically feel tired and depleted. One way to maintain a harmonious flow of energy and prevent the onset of disease is to practice a form of self-acupressure that we call CHI-ROBICS.

Practicing CHI-ROBICS will help you strengthen your immune system by maintaining a healthy flow of vital energy, or chi (pronounced chee), throughout your body/mind/spirit. This self-initiated balancing process stimulates the production of anti-bodies, white cells, and other components of your immune system.

Here is a simple exercise from CHI-ROBICS that takes only a minute to do:

Rub your hands briskly together for about ten seconds. Feel the warmth and energy (you may feel this as a tingly sensation) in your hands. Now, with the tips of your fingers, tap briskly all over your skull and the back of your neck for about fifteen seconds. This will feel something like the way water feels coming out of a show-erhead that has been set on strong pulse. Let yourself enjoy this feeling!

Again rub your hands briskly together, and this time gently rub your cheeks, nose, ears, and forehead with your open palms and with the pads of your fingers. Now stop, relax, and breathe. Sit down for a moment in a comfortable chair, and notice how you feel.

Beginning the Day with a Welcome

We learned this exercise from Dr. Leonard Laskow, an innovative holistic medical doctor living in California. It is a way of boost-ing the immune system by awakening an "attitude of gratitude" first thing in the morning. By embracing and welcoming the dawning day, one can cue the immune system to embrace life and stimulate it to produce antibodies and other factors that protect our health.

This exercise is ideally suited to the needs of the recovering addict, in that it is an antidote for feelings of hopelessness or stagnation by affirming the new life that dawns upon us with the awakening of each new day.

Ideally, do this exercise first thing in the morning. As you face the rising sun, take several full, easy breaths. Then, with arms raised upward toward the heavens, say the following aloud (preferably with vocal enthusiasm; it's OK to shout it!):

> *I welcome the sun.*
> *A new day has already begun.*
> *I welcome the sun shining above.*
> *Thank you for your light.*
> *Thank you for your love.*
> *I welcome the sun.*
> *A new life has just begun.*
> *Thank you! Thank you! Thank you!*

Taking an Earth Walk

Now take a walk on a very special planet . . . the earth! (If you are physically unable to walk, go for a ride in your wheelchair if you can, or ask someone to assist you. Otherwise, position yourself near a doorway or window, as close to the outdoors as possible, and do the exercise using your creative imagination.)

The purpose of this walk is for you to connect the source of healing at your own core with the powerful source of healing deep within Mother Earth. This way, you and the earth become a conscious team, co-creating a power boost for your immune system.

Take a moment to remind yourself of your choice to enjoy being healthy, and allow that choice to guide you in this exercise, in which you deliberately feel your feet more fully as you walk upon the earth.

Walk slowly and leisurely, and with each step feel the bottoms of your feet touching the earth. Notice your surroundings, and in particular feel your appreciation for whatever it is that strikes you as beautiful . . . colors, plants, trees, homes, children playing, a flag dancing in the wind. (You may even want to say an inner "Thank you!" for each thing that you appreciate, as described in chapter 5.)

Remind yourself that on this walk, there is nowhere to get to. You are already there, exactly where you need to be. Healing is available in each step. Listen through the soles of your feet . . . not with your mind and your physical ears, but with your heart . . . with the ears in your feet . . . with *all* of you.

Listen . . . feel the bottoms of your feet touching the earth . . . listen *deeply* . . . listen playfully . . . simply enjoy being at home . . . on your home planet!

Touch Can Heal

When we know that we are loved and touchable, our immune systems perform optimally. In particular, when we allow ourselves to *feel* loved and *receive* the love that is expressed to us, we give ourselves this message on a very deep level: "It is OK to thrive!"

This translates into healthy immune function. In many studies—among them those done at the University of Miami on premature human infants and at Ohio State University on rabbits—the extraordinary (though in another sense, quite ordinary) healing power of touch has been demonstrated.

In the Miami studies, premature infants gained weight 50 percent faster when they were held for fifteen minutes three times a day, as compared with those who were not held. In the Ohio study, rabbits that were touched and held by a lab assistant were more resistant to the development of heart disease, even though they were fed the same high-fat diets as the other rabbits in the study, who did go on to develop heart disease.

Our hunch is that, had it been looked at, the studies would have demonstrated that the health of those who *did* the touching also benefited.

Both touching and being touched strengthen immunity and promote health, as long as a loving intention is present.

We suggest that you use the healing power of touch to your advantage. Have a massage, either from a professional or as an exchange or sharing between friends. It needn't be done perfectly. Just volunteer to massage a friend's hands, or feet, or back. Or ask for healing touch from someone you trust and feel safe with.

Or simply share a hug. Or two. Or seven!

Of course, only engage in touching with people with whom you feel safe and whose intention to be unconditionally loving is clear to you. This helps create a safe environment, a sacred healing space in which both people feel honored and loved.

One way that you can give the gift of touch to yourself is to place one hand lightly on your forehead and the other hand lightly on your belly, just above your navel. Leave the hands in place for a few seconds, or even for a few minutes. Notice the sense of calm, healing, and protection that comes forth when you do this.

You can offer this simple method of touch healing to anyone who may need calming or loving support, including your children or other family members (or you can teach them to do it for you). This gift of touch is something you have with you all the time. Share it!

Healthy Boundaries

As we have discussed, one of the immune system's primary functions is to help maintain good health by defending against a wide variety of stressors encountered in everyday life. To be of optimal service to the individual, the immune system must be an effective protector—a potent defender of healthy boundaries.

One essential function of the immune system is to distinguish what is self from what is other. Only by making that distinction can the immune system know what to defend against and what to let be. For example, the immune system must know that the cells lining the respiratory passages are self, but that the potentially harmful influenza virus is other.

A failure of the immune system to recognize self as safe and nonthreatening can result in a health-destroying attack. This is precisely what occurs in so-called autoimmune diseases such as rheumatoid arthritis, ulcerative colitis, and lupus.

People in recovery often have personal boundary issues and typically become entangled in other people's lives in dysfunctional, co-dependent ways. It is important, therefore, that they learn to distinguish what is self from what is other on all levels, from the interpersonal to the intracellular.

Here is an exercise that uses the power of the mind and the creative imagination to coach the immune system in its important role of accurately distinguishing self from other. This guided imagery is best done in a quiet room, free of distractions. You may want to record it on tape or have someone read it to you.

In a comfortable seated position, close your eyes and bring
your attention to your breath. As you observe the natural
flow of the breath—without trying to change it in any
way—become aware of your heartbeat. Recognize that this is
your heart beating—*your* heart, lying deep within your
chest—fulfilling its natural function of pumping blood
throughout your body every moment of your life, day in
and day out.

Allow yourself to feel very grateful for your heart and
the life-giving function that it serves. Your heart is a part of
you—it *is* you. Receive and welcome your heart-full self.

Now, place both hands lightly on the front of your
chest and notice how your hands feel. As you feel your
hands touching the front of your chest, you feel your own
skin, the skin that covers the front of your chest, more easily. You feel this boundary between what is inside your body
and what is outside.

Notice how good it feels to know what is you: what is
inside you and what is outside you.

Not only your heart, but all the organs inside your
skin are part of you . . . your lungs and kidneys and liver . . .
your stomach, intestines, and brain . . . all the muscles,
bones, and connective tissue . . . all the arteries and veins.
They're all part of you, all part of your healthy, loving community within. Each one is your ally. All of them are your
personal helpers.

Consciously welcome each part of you by saying an
inner "Thank you" to all the bones, all the muscles, the
whole vast network of arteries and veins and nerves, even
the parts that you may not even know are there. Thank
them, too, for serving you, for taking care of you so well!
Consciously include them as part of your team of inner
healers, each part knowing just what to do, every cell doing
its special part to assist you, lovingly, wisely.

Outside of you is a whole vast world of others—people,
animals, minerals, plants, mountains and oceans, earth and

sky—all for you to relate to, however you may choose to interact with any of them. So *celebrate* the world that is outside of you; give thanks for the existence of that world.

And choose to receive from that world only what is good for you, only what serves you, only what is for your highest good—knowing that your choice is powerful, that you can have it be this way, safely, completely, just by deciding to make it so.

And now, if you haven't already done so, release your hands, removing them from the front of your chest and letting them float down, comfortably, into your lap. Take a few moments simply to enjoy being alive as *you!*

Now gradually open your eyes and take a fresh look at the world around you. Notice how you feel now, in this precious moment of your life.

Focusing on What You Love

As we've already discussed, your immune system is under the direction of your thoughts, your emotions, and the mental images that you focus upon. Too often, individuals in recovery engage in "stinking thinking," as it is generally called in twelve-step circles. This attitude of viewing oneself as a helpless victim and then focusing upon the hopelessness of a situation is an excellent way to undermine immune function.

> **Remember: You are in charge! Your antibodies and white cells are poised and ready to say "Yes!" to whatever you tell them to do.**

Another way to say this is: *What you focus on is what you get.* Wherever you place your attention, your immune system behaves accordingly.

Try this exercise. Use it to improve your health by translating your desire to live and to love into the physiological language of your immune system.

Find a quiet place where you feel safe and at home, somewhere that you can feel at peace and where you won't be interrupted by the telephone or other demands of daily life. Just be with yourself. Settle in and ask yourself this question: *What do I love?*

Now, in the privacy of your inner awareness, spend some time answering that question for yourself. Just let your attention meander freely as you allow yourself to focus on and feel whatever comes into your conscious awareness in response to that question.

Allow your attention to float from one image to the next, being sure to *feel* your love for that living being, thing, activity, situation, or idea.

Practice this exercise daily. If you like, you can write down whatever comes to you in a journal book or on a piece of paper.

Healing Herbs

Many healing herbs have immune-enhancing properties. These include echinacea, goldenseal, astragalus, and Siberian ginseng, among others. A whole array of Chinese and Ayurvedic (East Indian) herbs are also known to enhance immune function, though their names, properties, and specific uses are largely unknown except to traditional Chinese and Indian doctors.

A detailed description of immune-enhancing herbs and their specific healing properties is beyond the scope of this book.

We recommend that the recovering addict make judicious use of the healing properties that botanical medicines contain.

One way she can do this is to include in her daily regimen a liquid extract or capsules of freeze-dried herbs, which contain a combination of immune-enhancing herbs. Botanical medicine of this kind can be obtained at any reputable health foods store or directly through a supplier/manufacturer of such extracts (see Resources chapter). Because these extracts often contain alcohol, which may be unsuitable for those in recovery, a non-alcohol-based product (for example, a product extracted with glycerin) may be obtained.

One product that we have used to good benefit over the years is Immune Herbal Formula, a combination of about a dozen immune-enhancing herbs, extracted and distributed by Natural Herbal Essences (see Resources).

Because herbal products vary greatly in potency, we cannot specify an optimal daily dose without knowing the specific product used. However, our experience with using good-quality herbal extracts suggests that one-half to one dropperful (ten to twenty drops) daily is adequate for health maintenance in most situations.

An "A" for Ascorbic Acid

Taking vitamin C (ascorbic acid plus bioflavonoids) supports the health of the immune system. With our current cultural eating patterns and methods of food distribution and storage, it is nearly impossible for anyone to obtain adequate amounts of vitamin C from diet alone. This is particularly true for the recovering addict, whose eating patterns are often erratic, food choices poor, and stress levels, both from dietary and a variety of other sources, characteristically high.

We recommend that a daily vitamin C supplement be taken by anyone in recovery. How much is optimal? Since the answer to that question varies from individual to individual, as well as with the levels of stress that she may be experiencing, we suggest erring on the side of taking plenty. The risks of overdoing it are far outweighed by the benefits of getting enough. For most people, any excess will be safely excreted in the urine.

Being water-soluble, vitamin C is best taken in divided doses throughout the day or in a time-release form. We recommend a dosage range of 1,000 to 2,000 mg daily for most people.

One easy way to maintain an intake of vitamin C throughout the day is by using chewable vitamin C tablets, many of which have a pleasant, fruity taste. Keep a small container of them in your pocket or your purse, at your desk, and/or on the kitchen counter. Choose tablets that contain 250 to 500 mg of vitamin C and chew one every few hours, or whenever you happen to think of it. (There's no need to be religious about the dose. Just follow your instincts and aim for a total daily dose of up to 2,000 mg.)

Taking vitamin C daily is a simple, inexpensive way to promote well-being and strengthen your natural defenses against illness. (If you should experience upset stomach or diarrhea when taking vitamin C, which does occur for a small percentage of those who use it, try taking it with food, or choose a buffered form of the vitamin.)

Your Mission Statement

What do you want? What is the purpose of your life, as you see it? You'll find that when your life is "on purpose," your immune system will be healthy and on track.

> **Knowing what you want your life to be—especially developing a passion for living—automatically enlists your immune system in supporting your health and your life's mission.**

Right now, give some thought to what is most important to you. What makes your life worthwhile? What do you want for yourself? What talents do you want to express? What contribution do you want to make to the well-being of others and to the health of our planet?

> **When you focus on the particulars of your life's mission, you direct your awareness to the realm of possibility. You acknowledge the real potential that you have . . . to live the life of your heartfelt dreams.**

Right now, write a brief mission statement, a sentence or two about what you want your life to be and how you want to be investing your energy. What are your dreams, your highest aspirations? What are your healthy passions? What would you like them to be? What inspires you?

Begin with the words "I want" or "I choose." This is your statement of how you see your life mission *at this time.* Let it be subject to change as you and your intentions continue to change and evolve.

You may find that you'll want to do the exercise again, perhaps soon, just to see what may have changed for you. For now, read this mission statement daily to remind yourself of what is most important in your life and what you are aiming for.

The health of your immune system is the result of many different factors. Your ways of eating, thinking, and visioning all have an important impact. Your choice of living environment, your personal relationships, how you exercise, and your way of participating in our planetary community all play their parts, too.

Your immune system is always listening in, taking its cue from whatever your choices and attitudes convey about your life and how you want to live it. So practice telling yourself—and your immune system—the truth about what you want to create, for yourself and for the world . . . and *go for what you really want!*

10

Dreamwork

We are such stuff as dreams are made of.

—Shakespeare, *The Tempest*

The word *dream* is related etymologically to the ancient Anglo-Saxon word *dream*, which means "joy, music, and minstrelsy." It is also related to the word *ghost*.

Thus, one can view dreams as the means to make music out of the visible and the invisible realms, the known and the unknown. Each dream has the potential to help us invoke a special music that can harmonize these realms and bring greater joy and meaning into our lives.

As we travel recovery's marvelous road, we begin to reclaim lost parts of ourselves. We begin to live more consciously as we become more fully aware of the multiple dimensions of who we are.

Working with our dreams is a way of bringing our sacred ghosts, those formerly lost parts of ourselves, more fully

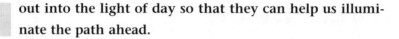
**out into the light of day so that they can help us illumi-
nate the path ahead.**

Many clients report that they've not remembered their
dreams for years. Others dream quite regularly. In both cases, we've
found that by engaging in conscious dreamwork our clients can
enhance their recovery process.

With addiction, toxicity itself can distort the dream life. It can
block the expression of dreams. When an addict begins to sober
up, he starts to awaken from the sleep of his "chemical cloud of
unknowing" as the central nervous system begins to return to
more normal functioning.

During the first few months of recovery, vivid, sometimes
nightmarish dreams are not uncommon. Because clients may not
have experienced such vivid dreams when they were sober, some
become frightened and confused by the intensity of their dreams.

Relapse dreams (that is, those in which the dreamer experiences a scenario of relapse in the dream itself) are a common
occurrence in all stages of recovery, though they tend to be most
frequent during the first few years of sobriety. Relapse dreams can
be terrifying. The dreamer often awakens believing she has had an
actual relapse—accompanied by the same guilt, shame, and despair
associated with the real thing.

A colleague of ours commented that she considers these
relapse dreams to be a useful gift. The person in recovery becomes
reminded through the dream of the painful reality of a potential
relapse. In the dream, he experiences all of what can and often
does happen in real life, but (thankfully!) without having to pay
the penalty of really going through it.

**Relapse dreams can be sobering reminders of addiction's
tenacious hold on the psyches of recovering addicts. As
reminders of what can be, they often serve as deterrents
to any lingering tendencies toward substance abuse.**

Many indigenous peoples look upon dreams with reverence. For them, dreams provide a map of what has been, what currently is, and what might occur in the future. Dreams are looked upon with respect for the wisdom they contain, information that's of value not only to the individual but for the community as a whole.

Our experience with clients in recovery has been that many have little or no recall of their night dreams. When they do remember, they often feel that the dream content is somehow not theirs. It often feels to them that someone else is speaking a strange foreign language. Consequently, they typically discard their dreams as valueless.

And yet, dreams can be a rich treasure trove of unconscious material that can facilitate recovery. They are like "windows to the soul" that can provide the dreamer with astonishing glimpses of the vast uncharted territory within himself.

We view dreams as emissaries of the soul. Like poetry, dreams speak through metaphor and symbolic imagery. The events of time and space are woven together in new and typically nonlinear combinations that appear on the surface to be illogical—even bizarre—and yet every dream contains a gift, a kernel of wisdom, a jeweled mirror through which the dreamer can learn to see her life more clearly.

Clients in recovery who have been willing to honor and work with these messengers from the unconscious have discovered how dreamwork can have a profound impact upon their growth and development as sober men and women.

Years ago, while presenting at a dream conference, Norman Bradford, a professor of Jungian dream analysis at the University of Maryland, made the statement we quote below. Since then, we have come to cherish and embrace this point of view in the dreamwork that we do with our clients (as well as in our own personal dreamwork). This perspective on what dreams are—for the individual and as a community resource—is the holy well we drink from, over and over again, in the dreamwork we do:

> Dreams are a sacred gift presented to us in the midst of our sleeping consciousness. Remember your dreams. Honor your dreams. Learn from your dreams.

Share your dreams with yourself and one another, for the world we live in truly needs your dreams.

The Gifts of Dreamwork in Recovery

Here are some of the ways that dreams can be of value to those in recovery:

1. Dreams help us discover and reclaim our shadow and make meaning out of the unconscious parts of our being. Much of the journey in recovery involves reclaiming parts of our lives—and ourselves—from which we have been estranged during the active phase of addiction.

2. Dreams help us see and recognize our limiting patterns more clearly, so that we can come to understand and know ourselves better.

3. Dreams awaken us to realms of enchantment, mystery, and the sacred.

4. Dreams provide us with a map to our inner world and offer us messages and instructions for living more consciously in sobriety.

5. Dreams can be a catalyst for change and a road map to choices that can have a profound impact on our future.

6. Dreams can help us feel more connected to both our inner and outer worlds.

7. Learning the primordial language of dreams can be fun, providing a new lens for seeing, understanding, and living a sober life.

Here are some perspectives on the nature of dreams and how one can best utilize them:

1. Treat every dream as a gift from your Higher Self.

2. All dreams are sacred and every dream has a message.

3. Dreams speak to us in symbols that can be both personal and archetypal in nature.

4. Rather than judge the content of a dream as good, bad, wonderful, or awful, let the dream stand on its own merit and speak for itself. Often, the most mundane dreams or seemingly horrible nightmares provide profound opportunities for learning about ourselves and about life in general.

5. Some dreams are more accessible and come through more clearly than others, so content yourself with remembering whatever you do. Even tiny fragments of dreams remembered can serve as shining jewels of insight and awakening.

6. It's not necessary to employ a dream analyst or follow a particular school of dream interpretation. To receive the benefits, all that's required is your willingness to stay open to remembering your dreams and your choice to value and to "listen" to them.

7. It's helpful to record your dreams and to share your dreams with others. When you record or share your dreams, always

use the present tense; for example, "I am walking down a road as the sun is beginning to set." Using the present tense helps make the dream more immediate and alive. It connects you more powerfully with the dream's unfolding story.

8. Every dream is a reflection of yourself. Every person, symbol, and theme that appears has a particular meaning and message that is relevant to your life.

   Remember that you are the author of your dreams. Whatever interpretations others, even therapists and other experts, may make, you always have the inside track on the dream's essence. You have the final word on the wisdom, the meaning, the message of your dream.

9. Be patient and proceed slowly as you work with your dreams. Especially pay attention to your affect/feelings in the dream so that you will not bypass the feeling dimension of the riches being presented.

The center that I cannot find is known to my unconscious mind.

—W. H. Auden

Over the years, we have drawn liberally from the dreamwork methods and principles of John Weir, as taught to us by a brilliant and devoted student of his work, our wonderful guide and friend Donna Lee Graham. This style of dreamwork is generally referred to as the Percept Orientation method.

What especially appeals to us about this approach to dreamwork is that every dreamer is given the opportunity to access the wisdom of his own dreams without the therapist or dream partner interfering or projecting her own interpretations onto the dream. This process often generates deep insights and awareness as the dreamer plumbs the depths of each dream, exploring its essence.

In this dream process, the dreamer circumvents the judging mind and dives deeply into the heart and marrow of the dream itself. Through this immersion, the dreamer more readily discovers the meaning and power of the dream.

This method, in which all dream material ("the good, the bad, and the ugly") is considered valid and worthy of investigation, is particularly well suited to people in recovery. It supports them in taking an honest look at all aspects of what their unconscious minds may be trying to bring to their attention.

Here's an example of the healing and transformative power of dreams, told to us by a client who was just beginning her second year of recovery. The recovery process in therapy often involves exploration and reclaiming the parts of one's being that have been hidden, lost, misplaced, or covered over by the toxic cloud that addiction generates in the human psyche.

The first one to three years of sobriety are often referred to as the early stages of recovery. Carlotta had never worked with dreams before, but she had a dream that was so vivid and disturbing that I invited her to experiment with the Percept Orientation method of processing dreams. The results were dramatic as she made crucial discoveries about her life that she was initially unable to access due to the intensity of the dream and the recent death of her mother.

Carlotta was in the process of radical change. Her art studio had burned to the ground, her parents had recently died, and she was in the process of trying to find a way to reinvent herself and her life. She was beginning to discover a lot about herself—what she really wanted in life, what her genuine gifts were. The last two months had been particularly poignant: She had met "the man of her dreams" and she was feeling on the verge of radical breakthroughs in her personal life.

In therapy, Carlotta had complained about feeling stuck, depressed, and lonely. Then, in one of her sessions, she presented the following dream about exhuming the body of her deceased mother, who had died fourteen months earlier.

Carlotta's dream had been profoundly disturbing to her and had left her feeling shaken. With it, she had tapped into a deep reservoir of sadness, grief, and horror. The dream had felt so real and so vivid, in fact, that she had been unable to grasp its meaning, having been so overwhelmed by the powerful emotions that accompanied it.

Carlotta had never worked with her dreams prior to entering therapy. Now, with our guidance, she explored this dream using the Percept Orientation method.

Here is the text of the dream in Carlotta's own words, followed by our commentary:

Exhuming the Body of My Dead Mother

I am in a house with some friends, maybe just people, as I don't know their names or faces. While we are standing around, a crew arrives to exhume my mother's body. We are all standing around watching, when someone suggests that we go for a walk and not watch the digging.

They have a big backhoe to dig with. After a few minutes we return, and to my surprise (astonishment) I see my mother's coffin sitting on the ground maybe forty or fifty feet away, with the lid open. I can plainly see my mother lying there, with her head facing toward me. I look down at my mother, who shows no signs of decay even though I know she's been in the ground for fourteen months!

I do not cry. I don't feel any emotions at all. She looks so peaceful. Then I wake up and realize it is a dream. At that point, I feel very sad and disturbed.

By delving into her dream with our guidance, Carlotta soon came to realize that this was not only a dream about her mother. Its theme was more about meeting parts of herself in a neglected and nearly forgotten part of her being (house), along with other parts of herself that she did not recognize (unknown friends).

She saw that in the dream she was unearthing an older, feminine part of herself that she loved and valued dearly (mother). To accomplish this, she had to engage powerful parts of herself (backhoe) to dig up and bring to the surface some parts of her being that had been buried.

In recognizing these aspects of the meaning of her dream and coming to understand the dream's deeper (though formerly hidden) message, Carlotta felt more at peace.

In a practical sense, she saw that the possibility of her having a life-mate, which she had told herself was "dead and buried" along with her mother, was in fact very much alive. She realized, too, that she need no longer fear the unknown. To the contrary, she could depend upon her formerly unrecognized inner resources to assist her in her journey, and to offer her delicious insights that would nourish and support her future successes.

By working with this dream, Carlotta moved with astonishing speed toward the actualization of some heartfelt "waking dreams" that had in the past eluded her. She reported feeling a strange, yet reassuring sense of power and wholeness emanating from somewhere deep within her soul.

Carlotta used this dream as a touchstone for the next six months as she slowly but surely reclaimed many cherished parts of herself that had become covered over but which now were becoming visible again. This dream helped her recognize, too, some ways that she had buried her creativity and her identity as an artist during the traumatic episode of losing her pottery studio—and to see that it was now a fertile time to make a fresh start.

In essence, this dream, which had originally felt like a traumatic nightmare, became transformed through dreamwork into a living catalyst for Carlotta's recovery and rebirth as an artist. It also fueled her awakening desire to pursue the important love relationship that was now unfolding in her life.

Recovery is a transformative process in which a person begins to reform and reshape an identity as a sober man or woman. Carlotta's dream was transformative in that it helped her recognize ways in which she had felt blocked—both as an artist and in the realm of love relationships—and this dream served as a bridge that began to open up new pathways in her life.

Dreamwork Exercises and Suggestions

Remembering Dreams

Some people remember their dreams quite readily. For others, the capacity to recall dreams must be developed. Our experience has been that even those who tell us that they virtually never recall their dreams can easily learn to do so.

It is especially helpful when the recovering addict has a clear intention to recall his dreams. One way he can do this is by making a deliberate choice to enjoy remembering his dreams, by saying the following, either silently or aloud, before going to sleep: "I choose to enjoy remembering my dreams when I awaken in the morning."

This conscious choice will seed the process of remembering and will facilitate the ease of dream recall. By repeating it every night for a few days or weeks, the individual will often begin to remember his dreams . . . maybe only snippets or vague impressions at first. Practice is the key!

It's helpful, too, to keep a blank pad of paper and something to write with by the bedside, so that dreams can be written down as soon as the dreamer awakens, before they slip away. We do not recommend harsh alarm clocks, which tend to jar the sleeper awake and interfere with the process of dream recall. If an alarm clock must be used, choose one that's more gentle, or find one that awakens you with soothing music rather than a harsh, jarring tone.

Experiment with a Voice Recorder

An inexpensive mini-cassette recorder can be purchased and kept by the bedside. Dreams can then be recorded simply by speaking them into the recording device. This can be an invaluable tool for assisting dream recall. During the night, reach over, grab the recorder, and whisper the dream into it. Then, when you get up in the morning, the dream will be there waiting for you, so that you can listen to it and record it in your dream journal (see below).

Typically, this method allows the dreamer to capture the dream in much greater detail. And if she shares a bed with someone, this approach has the added advantage of protecting her partner's sleep.

Keep a Dream Journal

Whether you jot down your dreams or record them on tape, it is helpful to transcribe them into a journal that you've designated solely for that purpose. Recording your dreams on paper often helps in identifying recurring patterns and themes. When you transcribe the dream, always use the first person, present tense.

> **We suggest that you relate to your dreams as living beings whom you have met in the dream life, and from whom you can learn invaluable lessons about how to conduct your waking life.**

Take a Specific Action in Honor of the Dream

In many cultures it is customary to acknowledge the gift of having received a dream by taking some specific action in honor of the dream. This action may or may not relate to the dream's literal content.

For example, if you dream about a cup of tea, you might make a cup of tea for yourself when you awaken and then affirm, "I now drink this cup of tea in honor of last night's dream." If you dreamed about a friend or a loved one, you might telephone that person or mail a note, again making a choice such as, "I choose to enjoy taking this action in honor of my dream."

You might take some generic action such as lighting a candle in honor of the dream. Or you might consciously link some mundane action, something that you'd be doing anyway, with your intention of honoring the dream: "This morning, I wash my face . . . I make my breakfast . . . I start my car . . . in honor of last night's dream." Honoring a dream in this manner is one innovative way to "nourish and water your dream gardens" so that they can continue to flourish, providing you with a ripe harvest of dream material to feed your recovery process.

Create a Dream Group

A dream group can provide a wonderful opportunity for friends to share and explore their dreams. Our experience has been that as participants learn more about one another and about themselves through sharing their dreams, some indefinable yet powerful bonding takes place among the group members.

It's best to meet at least once a month for a couple of hours. We've found four to eight participants to be a good size. (If you prefer, it is fine to meet at times as a group of two and share your dreams with just one other person.)

We recommend that the group be leaderless. Sit in a circle and light a candle in the center. This dream candle symbolizes the living beings that dreams are and the group's shared intention to illuminate their powerful messages.

Here are some instructions and guidelines to help you get started:

1. One person starts by presenting a dream, using first person, present tense. For example, "I am swimming in the ocean and I see a dolphin."

2. Just before he begins to describe his dream the presenter always says the following words: "I have myself be in a visioning part of me and I have that part be a dreaming part of me."

3. The one presenting the dream continues on, uninterrupted. This is not an occasion for interpretation by others in the group, but rather a time for the narrator of the dream to come to his own conclusions and insights through this lucid telling of the dream, which is facilitated by the sacred space that the group ambiance creates.

4. When the narrator of the dream has finished, others in the group may make comments or ask questions. (We have found that in general, the less "interpretation" by others, the better.) In commenting on the dream's meaning, the participants must own any interpretations they may make as their projections by using the specific wording, "In my dream, I . . ."

   That is, the dream, having been spoken aloud by the one who dreamed it, has now become a community resource. In a sense, it is now everyone's dream, co-owned by all members of the group and having the particular meaning given it by each individual.

5. Confidentiality is essential. This allows participants to feel more at ease and more willing to present dreams that are sometimes highly personal.

6. We recommend that dream group members do some basic reading beforehand on the dream percept approach. Especially recommended are writings by Donna Lee Graham and by John Weir.

7. Most important of all, have a good time! Dream groups can be richly rewarding and transformative for everyone involved—and a lot of fun in the process!

11

Tools for Transformation and Self-Reflection

Then the day came
when the risk
to remain tight in a bud
was more painful
than the risk it took
to blossom.

—Anaïs Nin

A fundamental premise of the clinical work we do is that each person is like a bud awaiting the right time to open and blossom. She already has within herself all the elements required for living an abundant, richly fulfilling life. It's just that these raw materials must be mined—accessed and refined so that she can truly show her mettle.

Our role as counselors, then, is to provide a safe, welcoming atmosphere in which personal transformation can occur.

The theologian Gustavo Gutiérrez once said, "I drink from many wells." As holistic health practitioners, we also drink from many wells, utilizing an interdisciplinary approach to healing that draws its sustenance from a diverse array of resources.

This chapter offers a sampling of what we call Tools for Self-Reflection. It includes information and strategies drawn from our experiences assisting clients in recovery in taking a more candid, introspective look at themselves, their progress, and their potential.

The Art of Journaling in Recovery

What lies behind us
and what lies before us
are tiny matters
compared to what lies within us.

—Ralph Waldo Emerson

We have found journaling to be an effective and valuable tool for our clients in recovery. Journaling provides a tangible, concrete channel for creativity and self-expression. By keeping a journal, an individual can learn to access deeper realms of conscious awareness.

Here are some of the specific benefits of journaling in the recovery process:

1. Through journaling we come to know ourselves better. We discover our depth more fully.

2. Journaling helps clients in recovery—especially those who may be overwhelmed by their feelings—identify and process those feelings and thoughts more easily and comfortably.

Through journaling, feelings that may have been blocked for years can surface in a safe way.

3. Keeping a journal provides the opportunity for individuals to track their growth and development. Especially at times of rapid growth and change, such as in recovery, journaling can provide a venue for examining the ebbs and flows of life. Patterns that might otherwise be difficult to discern can be perceived more easily.

4. Through journaling, an individual undergoing the dynamic process of change and self-discovery can catalogue the challenges, discoveries, learnings, and revelations taking place along the way.

5. The journal can be a valuable tool for organizing the flow of one's life into a manageable form as an ongoing personal inventory of the kind emphasized in twelve-step programs.

6. By tracking one's growth and daily progress in a journal, an individual in recovery can more easily identify warning signs, such as increased frustration, anger, and depression, that could signal a possible relapse.

7. A journal can be particularly useful for coping with highly charged feelings or conflicts. The tangible process of bringing pen to paper can itself be healing and centering. It can help bring clarity whenever there is turmoil.

8. Journaling helps people explore, access, and express their creativity.

Keep a journal in whatever way works best for you. Even five minutes at the beginning or the end of the day can be very helpful, though it is optimal to set aside larger blocks of time as this becomes possible. For some, journal writing comes easily. For others, it may be more of a challenge and a learned discipline. Most of our clients tell us that journaling brings them tremendous rewards.

Any notebook will suffice, but it is best to choose a journal that you find beautiful and appealing. Or you can create one that speaks to your heart and makes you smile. Some choose lined pages; others prefer unlined pages. One client chose to keep her journal on five-by-seven index cards, which she kept in a special box that she had designed specifically for that purpose.

Suggestions for Keeping a Journal

1. Once you've selected or created your journal, choose to make the writing process itself a sacred ritual. This is a special time that you've reserved just for you—to write and to express yourself. You might want to choose a particular desk or table as your journaling place and give it a special atmosphere or ambiance, for example, by lighting a candle before you begin.

2. Decide to be radically honest. Do not edit your writing. Just let it flow. Make it clear to your partner and to other family members that your journal is off limits to them. Some clients keep their journals in a computer file that has a special password. Others prefer to keep their journals handwritten, in a private place.

3. Be patient with yourself. Start slow and set realistic goals. Enjoy the process. Journaling need not be a chore. Find a balance between discipline and spontaneity.

4. You might want to read one of the following books. Each presents journaling in a way that is well suited to the needs of individuals in recovery: *At a Journal Workshop: Writing to*

Access the Power of the Unconscious and Evoke Creative Ability, by Ira Progoff, PhD., and *The Artist's Way: A Spiritual Path to Higher Creativity,* by Julia Cameron.

Keeping a Grace Map Journal

The unexamined life is not worth living.

—Thoreau

For many years, we've been captivated by the whole concept of grace and the astonishing impact that grace can have upon our daily lives. It seems that not a day goes by that does not surprise us with some gift of grace.

We define grace as "a gift presented to us by the universe that is free—that comes to us unbidden, with no strings attached." We have done nothing to earn these gifts, nor are we required to. They are offered to us, gratis, as a bonus for living on earth.

> **Grace is like a river that perennially flows through our lives. Our charge is simply to remain awake and conscious enough to notice and to enjoy the gifts being presented.**

Here's a story that illustrates how grace can appear unexpectedly, offering the raw materials out of which a potent insight can be woven:

> In 1993, on the winter solstice, Roger was standing on the deck of his retreat cabin in the Blue Ridge Mountains when all of a sudden a huge winter wind roared through the treetops. That wind blew a tiny bird's nest out of the trees. It landed at his feet.
>
> Roger looked down and picked up this miniature nest woven of green lichen, which had seemed to fall like a silent piece of sky. As he gazed at this jewel of creation that he was

now holding in his hand, he realized that it had been created by one of his favorite birds, the ruby-throated hummingbird.

As he marveled at the delicate beauty and intricate craftsmanship of this tiny nest, he began to think about the hummingbirds that had created it—birds that were like winged magicians that darted from flower to flower all day long, drinking nectar—so tiny, so fast, and so enchanting. He thought about the exquisite beauty condensed into such a small creature . . . and then began to smile as he realized that every human being has within himself, too, the same wondrous beauty as the hummingbird.

As he contemplated the gift of the hummingbird's nest that had literally fallen into his hands, he "heard" the following words:

Amazing Grace shines upon us like an ever-present rainbow. A river of Divine Light illuminates our meandering life journeys, dusting each of us with flashes of beautiful Light.

These gifts of grace serve as mirrors to our souls, awakening us to the ever-present power of Spirit in our daily lives. As we become more awake, we shine and glow like the iridescence of a hummingbird's wings in the sunlight.

One aspect of the recovery process whose value has too often been overlooked is the reawakening to life's magic, beauty, and grace.

In paying greater attention to the flow of grace and acknowledging its gift, with a nod of recognition or a prayer of gratitude, one's life becomes vastly enriched. A doorway to the heart opens.

Experiences of grace come in many forms. Some arrive quietly, like small droplets of gentle rain, while others may come crashing in upon us like huge, errant waves. Grace can be an opportunity to receive, in some totally unanticipated way; or to give, as one is unexpectedly called into service for one's fellow man, woman, or creature in the wild. Grace can often shake us, opening us to new ways of experiencing life.

The following exercise, which we suggest to virtually all our clients in recovery, was inspired by Roger's amazing grace experience with the hummingbird's nest. We call it a grace map journal.

But first, here are a few more examples of what we mean by everyday grace:

> Early one evening, while hiking in the Scottish Highlands, Barry found himself tired and alone, nearly at the summit of a three-thousand-foot mountain he had decided to climb rather late that day. He had been walking almost all day and had depleted the cache of food that he'd been carrying in his fanny pack.
>
> Now, he was famished, with another hour of hiking (mostly downhill, fortunately!) still ahead of him. When he arrived at the peak, he found an apple core lying on the ground. Whoever had eaten that apple must have done so casually, as there was still a lot of fruit left around the core.
>
> Barry ate the remainder of that apple, core and all! That meal, which he had fortuitously found in the grass, sustained him until he arrived, still hungry and tired, at the bed and breakfast where he was lodging.
>
> Barry remembers that humble apple core as one of the most delicious meals of his entire life.

> A client was driving to a hospital where her mother was scheduled to have surgery. She got caught in a dangerous thunderstorm on the freeway, which made her even more anxious and irritable than she had been.
>
> In the midst of this squall, sunlight appeared and a double rainbow illuminated the sky. The end of the rainbow appeared to be on the median of the freeway, so that the

woman actually drove through the prism of light on the road. The car itself became bathed in rainbow light. She drove for the remainder of the journey feeling peaceful and uplifted.

Once, while hurrying to work, Roger came screeching to a halt at a red light. As he was cursing his bad luck, he happened to look up into the trees and saw a red maple that looked as if it were on fire. Its beauty was awesome!

The red maple looked so vibrant that gazing upon it nearly took his breath away. That experience transformed his mood and set a tone of calm attentiveness that he easily maintained for the rest of the day.

One morning in early winter, while skating in the park, Barry saw an athletic-looking, white-haired man kneeling alongside the path. At first he thought nothing of it, but as he passed by, he heard a soft, plaintive voice calling out to him: "Will you help me?"

Barry quickly reversed his course and went back to investigate. The man was not injured—just frustrated and embarrassed because he was unable to tie his shoelace. It had come undone while he was walking, and because he had a sling on his left arm (he explained that he had broken his shoulder a few weeks earlier), he could no longer perform this simple maneuver that usually would have been second nature to him. Now, with the lace dragging precariously on the ground and his shoe riding loosely around his ankle, it was becoming very difficult for him to walk without tripping.

Although he was a grown man, in this situation he had been reduced to the status of a child. He needed his shoelaces tied. So Barry knelt down on the cold ground at the man's feet (appreciating the cushion from the cold that his knee pads provided—that itself was grace!) and tied the man's shoe, double-knotting it just to be sure. It looked as though the other lace might come undone, so he asked if he might retie that one, too.

The two men parted and shook hands. Barry left feeling buoyant and lighthearted at having received this gift of grace—an opportunity to have been of genuine service to a fellow human being in such a simple way. He had often skated in the park alone, wishing to make real contact with his neighbors instead of just waving hello, but he had been unsure of how to reach out. This time, grace had given him the invitation to meet a member of his family in loving, supporting community, and to bond in a special way.

One afternoon, Roger was hunting wild mushrooms. Frustrated at not having found even one mushroom, he became inattentive and tripped over a log. At first, this made him angry. But when he stood up his gaze was drawn to a beautiful purple color ahead of him on the forest floor. His irritability turned to curiosity.

When he walked over to have a look, he discovered there, in a beam of sunlight, one of the most beautiful wild orchids he had ever seen. When he looked more closely, he found that underneath the orchid was a prize edible mushroom, a fresh morel. Several dozen more of these delicious mushrooms could then be seen, flourishing very near the place where he was now standing.

Sometimes the face of grace isn't pretty. It comes in a package that shocks us—and yet, in retrospect, we come to recognize it for the gift that it is.

Charles, a man recently sober, tells this story. When he had finally returned to work and was feeling better about his life, he was out walking one afternoon in his business suit, quite proud of his return to responsible living.

He spotted a disheveled-looking young man digging through a dumpster in search of food. The man was wearing no shirt and had a whiskey bottle sticking out of his pocket. Thoroughly disgusted by what he saw, Charles took it upon himself to shoo the man away from the dumpster. Nonetheless, the man persisted in foraging for a meal. He could not be dissuaded. Just as this pathetic-looking man reappeared with his catch of leftover food, Charles had a vision in which he saw his own face superimposed upon the face of that desperate, lonely human being. He was moved to tears as he realized, "There but for the grace of God go I."

This event helped him anchor himself more fully along the path of recovery, with greater humility and deeper compassion for himself and for others.

The great poet-philosopher Johann Wolfgang von Goethe offered the following perspective on grace:

> Until one is committed, there is hesitancy, the chance to draw back, always ineffectiveness. Concerning all acts of initiative, there is one elementary truth, the ignorance of which kills countless ideas and splendid plans: In that moment when one definitely commits oneself, then Providence moves, too.
>
> Whatever you think you can do or believe you can do, begin it. Action has magic, grace and power in it.

Beginning to keep a grace map journal can have magic and power in it, too. By taking this simple action, a person in recovery who is willing to risk opening her heart to the healing power of grace can open new doorways of possibility.

Keeping a grace map journal is not an attempt to control the flow of grace. It is merely a way of recognizing more clearly the goodness, beauty, and love that are present.

The grace map journal fuels our aliveness and enhances our life energy. The more alive we feel, the less likely we are to return to drugs or alcohol, or to engage in other addictive behaviors that can limit or obscure our perception of the abundant flow of grace.

Directions for Keeping a Grace Map Journal

Select a journal or a special pad of paper.

Begin by deciding to become more open to seeing and experiencing your life in new ways. Each day, allow yourself to engage your awareness more fully as you notice the gifts of grace being offered to you. Simply pay attention.

Whether it is finding a parking space, a coin on the ground, or a helper angel who appears just at your time of greatest need, each time grace appears take a moment to acknowledge the gift being presented to you and let your whole being fill with gratitude. Say "Thank you" for the gift—to God, to the Universe, or to Grace itself.

Jot down in your grace map journal a brief description of each experience of grace that you've noticed.

Continue this exercise for several months and then set aside some time to read through what you have written in your journal. Pay particular attention to any shifts in perception that may have taken place or any insights that may have occurred to you—about how life is, how the world is, and how you are—during the time that you've been keeping the journal.

It can also be a powerful experience to share these experiences with a close friend or with a group. For example, on a number of occasions we hosted storytelling circles (see chapter 6 for more details) whose theme for the evening was "stories of amazing grace." At those gatherings, a group of close friends spent the evening in candlelight sharing their grace stories. Such occasions typically proved to be joyful and inspirational for those who attended.

> **When we are experiencing joy and gratitude, our immune systems are at their strongest. Our life energy becomes amplified. This enhancement of our overall health and vitality is part of the hidden grace that accompanies each of our grace moments.**

Many of our clients seem amazed by the frequency of grace moments in their lives, once they become tuned in to noticing them.

Here is one final story, an event that took place at a retreat we were facilitating some years ago for several dozen people in recovery. The topic for this weekend retreat was "Addiction and Grace."

We were introducing the concept of the grace map when our presentation was suddenly interrupted by a loud voice from the back of the room. "What is all this *bullshit* about grace? I don't know what the hell you're talking about with all these fancy words!"

We were a bit unnerved by the woman's sudden angry outburst, but we thanked her for her comments, nevertheless. We explained to her that grace could also be thought of as a kind of free gift that can arrive quite unexpectedly. The woman became quiet.

The next day, all the participants began the process of keeping a grace map journal, jotting down what they recalled of their own experiences of amazing grace. When the group reconvened on the last day to share their experiences, the woman raised her hand and proceeded to tell her story, which moved everyone deeply.

She described the many difficulties in her life, especially her persistent poverty, which frequently was terrifying for her. She said that she hadn't been able to sleep the previous night, as she tossed and turned in bed, pondering this free gift of grace thing. She had thought that "this kind of stuff only happens to other people."

But then she had remembered two experiences from the week before, which she now shared with the group. She told a story about having missed the late-night bus. Stranded in an unfamiliar, dangerous neighborhood, with no money and no way home, she had managed to find her way to a pay phone, but then realized that she had no money with her, only her bus pass.

Standing under the streetlight, and noticing that her shoelaces had become untied, she spotted a quarter on the ground. She was then able to call a friend and get a ride safely home.

A few days later, she had gone to the convenience store to buy a pack of cigarettes and had discovered that she was a few pennies short. A man whom she had never met seemed to appear out of nowhere and gave her the money she needed. She called these gift coins "pennies from heaven."

Finally, in concluding her story, she told us that though she still wasn't sure about all this "grace stuff," she wanted to let us all know that she was "warming to it." At that point, she got up, rushed out of the room, and left the retreat.

> *Chance is always powerful.*
> *Let your hook be always cast*
> *in the pool*
> *where you least expect*
> *there will be a fish.*

> —Ovid

What Ovid calls "chance" we prefer to call "grace."

We believe that whether you are a skeptic or a person of unshakable faith, your life will be warmed—even transformed—when you take note of these grace experiences and pay attention to the insights that spring from them.

Eleanor Roosevelt has often been quoted as saying that "it is always better to light one candle than to curse the darkness." Those in recovery know that life is not always easy, that recovery tends to be a very rocky road.

But by awakening to and honoring the flow of grace and goodness in our lives, we can profoundly change our perspective. Our choice is not to deny the darkness, but to focus more fully on the light in our lives.

Sanctuary Space: Creating a Retreat for Yourself

*For everything there is a season, and a time for every
matter under heaven:*

> *A time to be born, and a time to die;*
> *A time to plant, and a time to pluck up what is planted;*
> *A time to kill, and a time to heal;*
> *A time to break down, and a time to build up;*
> *A time to weep, and a time to laugh;*
> *A time to mourn, and a time to dance;*

A time to throw away stones, and a time to gather stones together;

> *A time to embrace, and a time to refrain from embracing;*
> *A time to seek, and a time to lose;*
> *A time to keep, and a time to throw away;*
> *A time to tear, and a time to sew;*

A time to keep silence, and a time to speak;

> *A time to love, and a time to hate;*
> *A time for war, and a time for peace.*

—Ecclesiastes 3:1–8

For many years, we have facilitated both weekend and daylong retreats for men and women in recovery. The themes for these retreats have varied, but one thread has permeated all our retreats: the perspective of a retreat as a *rest stop,* as a time to pause, listen, and reflect upon our lives, how they have been and how we now want them to be.

> **A retreat is intended as a time for gaining insight and perspective on whatever is most important. It is a blessed time of rest and renewal, an ideal time to review what has been as we reset our course along the road to recovery.**

We've found that most people in recovery have never experienced this kind of retreat. They've not made it a priority. In most cases, they've never even considered it. Yet, we've found that choosing retreat as a sacred opportunity for spiritual, physical, and psychological renewal can be one of the best decisions that individuals in recovery can make.

These days, many of us lead marathon-like lives. Our modern culture is so saturated with noise—visual noise, auditory noise, media overload—that it can be a challenge for us to escape all that by setting aside time for the sole (soul!) purpose of healing, rest, and renewal.

> **We all need to recharge our batteries from time to time. A retreat is often a wonderful way to accomplish this, a natural route for finding peace and balance.**

There are many retreat centers in the United States and around the world that one can attend for a day, a weekend, or even for a more extended time. Some centers request that silence be maintained; others allow talking. Most include the opportunity for some interaction with others.

We encourage our clients to take some time out of their often busy lives for a personal retreat, if at all possible. For some, this may mean spending half a day in a place they find sacred and beautiful, some specially chosen location free from the usual distractions such as clocks, phones, or television. A mini-retreat of this kind can take place in a park or some other suitable sanctuary space. It can even be held at home. Whatever location you select, the key to success is to create a time apart from the usual business of your life when you can simply *be present.*

Many recovering addicts derive enormous benefits from retreat time. In fact, a retreat can be the ideal time and place to attend to some of the formal inventory work that is an essential component of nearly all twelve-step programs.

Based upon our recommendation, many clients have taken a personal retreat every year, sometimes even twice a year. Here are some of the benefits they report:

- Rest
- Renewal
- Healing
- Spiritual growth
- Transformation
- Peace
- Joy
- Serenity
- Heightened awareness

Each year, as part of his recovery process, Roger has taken a five-day silent retreat in the mountains. Barry's way, on the other hand, has been to take several retreats of shorter duration, sometimes close to home, sometimes in other parts of the country or abroad. Here is Roger's description of the way in which a typical five-day retreat generally unfolds for him (Barry's retreats tend to be less structured, but the same intentions and spirit apply):

> First, I block off the time on my calendar. Because the retreat is very important to me, I guard this time and space. Prior to the retreat, I notify friends, family, and clients of my intentions, making sure that my whereabouts are known, should any emergencies arise. I leave an address and phone number where I can be contacted by a neighbor, or even by the police, if that should become necessary. Having carefully "covered my bases" in that way, I can now feel truly free.
>
> Most of my retreats have taken place at my home in the mountains. I prepare all my food ahead of time so that very little energy will be required for cooking during the retreat itself. I close the gate to the property and offer a prayer, asking that this retreat might be a sacred time for healing, renewal, and self-discovery.
>
> I then go into the house and create an altar with candles and seasonal items—leaves, flowers—native to the land itself. I carefully and mindfully set up a table for morning prayer, writing, and meditation practice.
>
> I unplug all the phones and the fax machine and hide all the clocks. I create no agenda, no plans, no structure other than preparing the space as I have described.
>
> This is my "sacred" time to wake up whenever I wake up, sleep whenever I am tired, and simply be as fully present as I can be, letting Spirit guide me.
>
> When the retreat is over, I always feel renewed and alive. Sometimes major breakthroughs have taken place, but typically the changes have been more subtle. In either case, I know that during my retreat I have planted seeds of mindfulness and healing that will sustain me in times ahead— and help me meet the challenges that will inevitably come my way.
>
> These five precious days have always turned out to be deeply healing and transformative. I cherish this time alone.

This retreat time has become an essential component of my personal health practice.

To conclude, here's our combined recipe for a renewal retreat:

- Choose a time that you can set aside solely for your retreat and for no other purpose.
- Choose a place that feels like a sanctuary. It can be your home, a retreat center, a bed and breakfast, or a park or garden. Put away all clocks, turn off telephones, and notify friends and family members of your intentions.
- Make sure that you are free from any unnecessary obligations, demands, and distractions such as telephone, television, fax machine, and the like.
- Provide simple food for yourself that requires little or no preparation. Or have your food provided by the retreat center staff.
- Bring a journal and writing implements—pens, felt-tip markers, and so on.
- If you choose to bring something to read, do not bring a book or other reading material that you would typically read at other times. Instead, choose the kind of book that you can read slowly and attentively as a meditation. Consider not bringing any reading materials at all, but taking a complete break from reading in favor of just enjoying the silence.
- Bring comfortable clothes and shoes, both for indoor use and for outdoor meanderings.
- Don't even consider working or doing chores on your retreat!
- Give yourself as much time on retreat as possible and certainly enough time to create a fulfilling retreat experience. We recommend at least half a day and preferably one full day or weekend.

Flower Essences in Recovery

In considering the merits of flower essences for treating individuals in recovery, we delve into an area that lies outside the boundaries of conventional medicine. Nonetheless, we have come to value flower essences as a kind of "energy medicine" that often benefits our clients.

We readily acknowledge that there is much that remains unknown (and that perhaps will never be fully understood) about the nature of healing and illness. In that spirit of exploration and humility, we approach the realm of flower essences to explore their potential as practical, beneficial tools for health maintenance and transformation.

In Barry's story of recovery from addiction to nicotine (chapter 2), he mentions using a mixture of Bach Flower Remedies prescribed for him by a pioneering colleague. That prescription of natural medicine played a key role in his subsequent healing, in which he broke free of the smoking habit within a few weeks and became a nonsmoker for life.

What are flower essences and how do they seem to work? Perhaps this is best expressed in the words of Machaelle Small Wright, who directs a research center near Warrenton, Virginia, in which humans work co-creatively with the natural world of animals and plants. At Perelandra, flowering plants are grown whose energetic essences are carefully extracted in a precise and exacting manner. These essences are then bottled for use by the general public. The instructions for their use, based upon Machaelle's extensive research and experience, are included with Perelandra's products.

According to Machaelle's description, the essences "are produced from the flowers, vegetables and herbs grown in the Perelandra garden." They are bottled in concentrate form in pharmaceutical dropper bottles and are used by taking a drop directly on the tongue or several drops in a glass of water to be sipped throughout the day.

A senior staff member at Perelandra says this about the Perelandra Flower Essences: "The essences are liquid, pattern-infused solutions made from flowers. Taken orally, they are used in the natural repair and balancing of the human biological-electrical system. Each essence contains a specific electrical pattern that can correct specific imbalances in humans."

And again in Machaelle Small Wright's words:

> Flower essences work directly with both the electrical and the central nervous systems. By taking the correct essences, we immediately balance the electrical system, stabilize the nervous system, and stop the domino effect that leads to illness.
>
> The key to this change is balance. The flower essences support and help secure balance on all levels—physical, emotional, mental, and spiritual.
>
> - Physically, they balance the body by reconnecting and adjusting the electrical system.
> - Emotionally and mentally, they help the person identify, alter, and sometimes remove emotional and mental patterns that challenge overall balance.
> - Spiritually, they assist the person's connection to and understanding of the many levels of self to be able to operate in life from a broader perspective.

Given these benefits and the fact that addicts, whether in recovery or not, have overly stressed nervous systems for a variety of reasons, we have recommended the use of flower essences to many of our clients. It is also worth mentioning that these essences (or remedies, as they are sometimes called) are totally safe. They will always do no harm and have no side effects whatsoever.

Flower essences are not designed to preclude any forms of conventional medical treatment that might be necessary. They are, however, a valuable tool that when used in conjunction with other treatments will support a person's health and healing process.

Flower essences, whether Perelandra, Bach, or others, are always available over the counter without a prescription. Some specialized drugstores may carry a limited selection, but most drugstores in the United States will not have them. You will find ways of obtaining them by mail order listed in the Resources chapter.

Perelandra provides a valuable alternative for individuals in recovery by offering their wide range of essences in an optional vinegar-based, as opposed to the more traditional alcohol-based, solution. Worthy of special mention is an individualized flower essence mixture developed at Perelandra called ETS (Emergency Trauma Solution). This solution is made up in advance and kept on hand for use during the first twenty minutes after an accident, sudden illness, or shock. We have found ETS to be highly effective, whether dealing with a physical injury, emotional trauma, or spiritual crisis. We keep a bottle of ETS in the glove compartments of our cars and always carry it as part of our first-aid kit whenever we're on the road. We encourage our clients to do so, as well.

We always keep a variety of both Perelandra and Bach flower essences on hand in our offices. We frequently test clients to find out which essences are appropriate to use on that particular occasion. Depending on what we find, we may administer them before, during, and/or after the session.

Because the process of recovery involves such a radical shift—physically, mentally, psychologically, and spiritually—beginning with substance withdrawal itself and extending into middle- to late-stage recovery, flower essences can provide a safe and viable means of supporting a person through that frequently traumatic process.

Here are some of the many benefits we've observed in using flower essences with recovering addicts:

- Stabilization of mood swings
- Greater willingness to tolerate the reawakening of feeling of all kinds (physical, emotional, sexual, etc.) that typically accompanies the radical rebirth of recovery
- Facilitation of the process of psychological/emotional/physical shifts and breakthroughs
- More graceful navigation of life transitions (separation/divorce, realignment of friendships, job and career changes, etc.) that frequently accompany the recovery process
- Balancing the nervous system and anchoring the body's electrical system, which may be evidenced, for example, by an increased ability to relax and focus one's attention, even while undergoing the profound shifts and changes that characterize the recovery process
- Easing the movement toward homeostasis from a state of chemical-induced toxicity into well-established sobriety

The large body of research data provided by Perelandra, coupled with our own personal and clinical experiences, has demonstrated to our satisfaction that flower essences have tremendous healing benefits. Their power in helping Barry overcome his long-standing addiction to nicotine is by no means an isolated occurrence.

Given their impeccable record for safety and the many potential benefits they may bring to the recovering addict, we do espouse the use of flower essences as an adjunct to other approaches we may be utilizing, including many of those described elsewhere in the book. Over the years, we have seen how these natural healing agents can both complement and enhance the potency of our other interventions.

12

Conclusion

Many moons ago, in a winter snowstorm in Rappahannock County, Virginia, this book came rolling in on the wings of grace, asking to be born. Now, nearly three years later—in the harvest season of October's glory, with flaming colors, dazzling landscapes, and crisp clear days—the book has been completed.

Putting Out the Fire of Addiction announced itself, and the seed was planted that day. It was nurtured during a series of secluded retreats that we took in the Blue Ridge Mountains. These weekend retreats were sacred times in which the gestation of *Putting Out the Fire of Addiction* could naturally take place. They provided us the blessed opportunity to let go of the extreme busyness of our personal and professional lives so that we could focus instead on the book's unfolding.

At every stage, the book showed us what its timing would be, and though we often railed at what seemed like an interminable process of birthing it, we knew that its eventual completion was inevitable.

Though we treasured our times on retreat, the writing of this book was more a continuous process. The spirit, or *deva,* of *Putting Out the Fire of Addiction* accompanied us everywhere as it took form within each of us wherever we happened to be. Along every step of that meandering journey—whether in the mountains of Virginia, the suburbs of Kensington, Maryland, the cliffs of southern California, or the green hills of Ireland—we dedicated ourselves to attracting and creating the sacred space in which to do our work.

When we were on retreat at our home base, we lit candles, filled the house with cut flowers from the gardens, and prepared simple, delicious meals that we ate mindfully and with profound gratitude. Sometimes we set up our laptop computers under huge pine trees, near gardens bursting with native flowers and feeders that attracted birds and other wildlife into our writers' sanctuary. Nearby were whimsical sculptures and shrines that we had erected to serve as living, ever-changing reminders of what we deem holy in our lives—that which we choose to honor in our lifestyles and in our work-styles.

Writing this book has been a long and sometimes arduous journey, at times exhausting, yet always inspiring. Our intention at every step has been to fully embody in our own lives the principles, practices, and tools that we have shared with you.

This book sprang from our real-life experiences as human beings and as health practitioners. We have written it in sacred partnership and genuine collaboration, as a co-creative expression of the best that we each have to offer, each of us energizing his heartfelt intention to create something that would be of real service to others as well as a joy for ourselves.

There is a saying in AA about "walking the talk." In ministry, "Practice what you preach." In medicine, "Physician, heal thyself."

This writing clearly reflects who we are and how we live and practice. We have poured our hearts and souls onto these pages and have candidly shared the essence of our practical philosophy of living.

At our retreat center there's an eleven-foot-tall outdoor sculpture by Thomas Fernandez called "Breaking Free." This sculpture, crafted from the steel hull of a discarded navy battleship, glows day and night with a rich, rust-colored patina. This imaginative sculpture features a see-through rendition of a man's silhouette that appears as a negative image. Crowning this life-sized work of art is the positive image cutout itself, of a man dancing in the wind, one finger lightly touching the silhouette from which he seems to have emerged, like a butterfly from its chrysalis.

"Breaking Free" celebrates the human spirit, which, having broken free from the prison of its former self, can now dance unencumbered in the wind as it celebrates new life in joy and newfound expression. The one finger touching the old see-through image of the man's body reminds us how essential it is that we keep in touch with our former selves and thereby honor the past—the pain, the struggles, and the suffering that we may have come through—and survived! It reminds us, too, that we have a perennial opportunity to heal the wounded parts of ourselves, and a responsibility to assist others who may be struggling to break free of their own self-limiting patterns.

Given this outlook, we wish to dedicate the sculpture "Breaking Free," along with its universal message, to all the men, women, and children who have faced the daunting power of their addictions, those who have already broken free or are in the process of doing so. May they all dance and celebrate life to the fullest of their God-given potentials.

We feel deeply indebted to the countless friends, clients, and others who have supported us in this writing. Thank you for affirming along with us that we are all one community on this great ship of life.

One of our reviewers, a retired physician living on the West Coast, made the following comment after reading the manuscript: "This book should not be reserved only for people in recovery from addictions. Addiction is part of being human, and my experience with this writing is that the message applies for all of us. We are all human beings *recovering from something* that has limited our capacity to be fully alive."

It is our hope and prayer that this book may serve as a beacon of light for men and women everywhere who are walking the sacred road to recovery.

We'd like to conclude with this healing story that began to unfold in our lives five years ago around the time of the winter solstice and which has culminated in the completion of this book on this rich autumn day on the threshold of the upcoming millennium. We call this story "One Green Leaf."

One day, while walking in the naked winter landscape, we each found a tiny oak leaf and held it in our hand. As we did this, we thought about the sacred lineage of those trees. With a spirit of reverence, we acknowledged the grandfather oak that provided us with these tiny leaves, now our living symbols of ancient wisdom.

We saw each leaf as a messenger from the heart of creation. We laughed like young children, and then we said a prayer of thanksgiving, as each of us put the leaf into his mouth.

As we chewed these slightly bitter leaves, we focused our attention upon this sacred truth—*that the entire Earth and all her creatures are nothing less than God's living flesh.*

Every time we enjoy a meal harvested from her living soils, every time we breathe her life-giving air or drink her pure, clean water, we are receiving and celebrating these gifts of holy communion.

Within even the tiniest plant and within every human being dwells a baby Buddha, the heart of Jesus, the love of Allah, the voice of Yahweh. Every stone, every squirrel, every molecule of air that we breathe is a living expression of God's generous Spirit.

Nature's communion comes in many forms—a mint blossom, a dewdrop, a chanterelle mushroom, a sprig of fiddlehead fern. Today, it's a tiny green leaf of the sweet oxeye daisy that we've taken as communion, with gratitude and pure delight!

Each green leaf harvested from nature's garden has within it the blueprint for all of creation—and *so do you!* The essence of life itself, so green, so fresh, and so alive, is housed within these leaves and within us all.

Like the green leaves we found five years ago as well as on this radiant autumn day, each person has a map within his soul that he can learn to read, a sacred blueprint for thriving and, ultimately, for *celebrating* the gifts of sober living.

We hope that you remain green and fresh as you journey both alone and in community along the road to recovering your true essence. We offer our blessings and gratitude to the entire sacred web of life. And we offer this healing prayer for all men, women, and children still suffering under the weight of addiction.

> May the light of recovery touch your heart and heal the broken fences within your being. May that powerful light also heal those whom you love. May you break free from the prison of addiction to touch, taste, and experience the freedom that awaits you in recovery.

YOU must be the light
you wish to see
in the world.

—Buddha

Resources for Recovery

Twelve-Step Programs

Adult Children of Alcoholics

International—more than 2,000 groups. Twelve-Step program designed to assist individuals raised in a dysfunctional environment with alcoholism or other family dysfunctions. ACA, P.O. Box 3216, Torrance, CA 90510; (818) 594-7248.

Al-Anon Family Groups

International—over 35,000 groups. Fellowship of men, women, and children whose lives have been affected by the alcoholic drinking of a family or friend. 1-800-344-2666.

Alateen

International—more than 5,000 groups. Fellowship of young people whose lives are affected by someone else's drinking. 1-800-344-2666.

Alcoholics Anonymous World Services, Inc.
International—more than 94,000 groups worldwide. Check your local phone directory for information regarding meetings. General Service Office, 475 Riverside Dr., 11th Floor, New York, NY 10115; (212) 870-3400.

Codependents Anonymous
International—more than 4,000 groups. Twelve-Step program designed to help people find freedom and peace in their relationships. P.O. Box 33577, Phoenix, AZ 85067; (602) 277-7991.

Gamblers Anonymous
International—more than 1200 groups. Twelve-Step program designed to assist people who are addicted to gambling. P.O. Box 17173, Los Angeles, CA 90017; (213) 386-8789.

Narcotics Anonymous
International—more than 25,000 groups. A fellowship of men and women modeled after AA but focusing on drug addiction. (818) 780-3951.

Nicotine Anonymous
International—more than 500 groups. Twelve-Step groups for recovery from nicotine (tobacco) addiction. P.O. Box 591777, San Francisco, CA 94159; (415) 750-0328.

Music for Meditation and Guided Imagery

Robert Gass and On Wings of Song

Beautiful extended-length meditative chants, cross-cultural, including titles such as "Alleluia," "Kyrie," "Om Namah Shivayah," and "Ancient Mother."

Inner Peace Music

Steven Halpern, 1-800-909-0707; www.stevenhalpern.com.

Daniel Kobialka

Classical violinist who has created music wonderfully suited for guided imagery and meditation. We have used these recordings extensively for group retreats and trainings. We particularly recommend "Rainbows" and "Going Home."

Ladyslipper Inc.: Recordings by Women

Excellent resource for recordings by women. Superb collections of CDs and tapes from female musicians such as Kay Gardner and Lisa Thiel. We especially recommend Kay Gardner's "Rainbow Path; Garden of Ecstasy" and "Moods and Rituals." P.O. Box 3124, Durham, NC 27715.

Mind/Body Medical Institute

Excellent-quality tapes for stress reduction, relaxation, pain management; based on the work of Herbert Benson, M.D. (617) 632-9525.

Mozart Effect Resource Center

Don Campbell, 1-800-721-2177.

Music of Hildegard De Bingen
"A Feather on the Breath of God" (and other titles). Exquisite and hypnotically beautiful music in the style of Gregorian chants.

Synchronicity Foundation
High-tech extended-length meditations drawn from many sacred traditions, utilizing sound patterning that facilitates transcendental experience and whole-brain healing. Titles such as "Ave Maria," "Om Namah Shivayah," "La Illaha Il Allah," etc. 1-800-962-2033; www.synchronicity.org.

Retreat Centers

There are thousands of retreat centers worldwide. For locating retreat centers in the United States, we recommend the following books:

Benson, John. *Transformative Adventures, Vacations and Retreats: An International Directory.* New Millennium, 1994.
Cooper, David. *Renewing Your Soul.* New York: Harper, 1995.
————. *Silence, Simplicity and Solitude: A Guide for Spiritual Retreat.* New York: Crown, 1992.
Kelley, Jack, and Marcia Kelley. *Sanctuaries: A Guide to Lodgings in Monasteries, Abbeys and Retreats in the United States.* New York: Crown, 1996. (Also see *The Whole Heaven Catalogue,* a resource guide to products and services of spiritual/ cooperative communities, by the same authors.)

Wellness and Self-Care

American Holistic Health Association
("The leading national resource connecting people with vital solutions for reaching a higher level of wellness")
P.O. Box 17400
Anaheim, CA 92817
(714) 779-6152
e-mail: ahha@healthy.net
www.ahha.org

American Holistic Medical Association
6728 Old McLean Village Dr.
McLean, VA 22101
(703) 556-9245
e-mail: ahma@degnon.org
www.holisticmedicine.org

Empowering Personal Wellness
www.onehealthyuniverse.com

Guided Imagery Resource Center (Belleruth Naparstek)
e-mail: imagerynews@healthjourneys.com
www.healthjourneys.com

G-Jo Institute
(Educational materials for acupressure and other self-help)
P.O. Box 1460
Columbus, NC 28722-1460
(828) 863-4660
www.g-jo.com

Eupsychia Institute (Jacquelyn Small, L.M.S.W.)
P.O. Box 3090
Austin, TX 78764
1-800-546-2795
www.eupsychia.com

HealingMatters™ (Barry Sultanoff, M.D.)
www.humormatters.com/healingmatters.htm

HealthWorldOnline
www.healthy.net

HumorMatters (Steven Sultanoff, Ph.D.)
www.humormatters.com

Project NatureConnect (Michael Cohen)
www.ecopsych.com

Sinus Survival (Robert S. Ivker, D.O.)
www.sinussurvival.com

Botanical Medicines (Herbs)

Two excellent sources of high-quality herbal extracts and other
preparations are:

Eclectic Institute
4385 SE Lusted Road
Sandy, OR 97055
1-800-332-4372

Natural Herbal Essences
432 Bolton Road
East Windsor, NJ 08520
(609) 448-8744

Flower Essences (and related topics)

Bach Flower Remedies
Nelson Bach USA, Ltd.
100 Research Dr.
Wilmington, MA 01887
1-800-319-9151
www.nelsonbach.com

Flower Essence Services
P.O. Box 1769
Nevada City, CA 95959;
1-800-548-6467
www.floweressence.com

Perelandra Center for Nature Research
P.O. Box 3603
Jeffersonton, VA 20188
1-800-960-8806 (within the U.S. and Canada)
(540) 937-2153 (all other countries)
fax: (540) 937-3360
www.perelandra-ltd.com

Perelandra is an extraordinary research center begun in 1976 that has developed an approach to healing called "co-creative science." Co-creative science is the study of man and nature working together in partnership as co-equals. We recommend Perelandra as a comprehensive resource center for flower essences, video and cassette tapes, and publications related to co-creative nature research.

In particular, read *Flower Essences: Re-Ordering Our Understanding and Approach to Illness and Health,* by Machaelle Small Wright (1988).

Other books by Machaelle Small Wright: *Behaving as If the God in All Life Mattered; Medical Assistance Program (MAP); The Microbial Balancing Program Manual; Perelandra Garden Workbooks.*

Resource Guides

Parallax Press Catalogue

Published by the Community for Mindful Living, this catalogue provides a comprehensive listing of books and audio/video based on the teachings of Thich Nhat Hanh. Excellent resources for meditation.

Simpkinson, Chuck, and Anne Simpkinson. *Soul Work: A Field Guide for Spiritual Seekers.* New York: HarperPerennial, 1998.

This is one of the most comprehensive resource guides for spirituality and personal growth. Extensive listings of resources related to spiritual psychotherapy, educational foundations and institutions, conference centers, interfaith resources for prayer/meditation, nutrition, literature, periodicals, and training institutes worldwide.

Sounds True Recordings
735 Walnut St.
Boulder, CO 80302
(303) 449-6229

Excellent source for audio tapes, books, and videos on meditation, transpersonal psychology, guided imagery, prayer, ritual, and dreamwork.

Other Recommended Books

Addiction and Recovery

Grof, Christina. *The Thirst for Wholeness: Attachment, Addiction, and the Spiritual Path.* New York: HarperCollins, 1993.

Larson, James. *Seven Weeks to Sobriety.* New York: Fawcett Columbine, 1997. A superb guide to the biochemical role of nutrition in the recovery process.

May, Gerald G. *Addiction and Grace: Love and Spirituality in the Healing of Addictions.* New York: HarperCollins, 1988.

Small, Jacquelyn. *Awakening in Time: The Journey from Codependence to Co-Creation.* New York: Bantam Books, 1991.

————. *Becoming Naturally Therapeutic: A Return to the True Essence of Helping.* New York: Bantam Books, 1990.

Sparks, Tav. *The Wide Open Door: The 12 Steps, Spiritual Tradition and the New Psychology.* Center City, Minn.: Hazelton Educational Materials, Inc., 1993.

Wilson, Bill, and Alcoholics Anonymous. *Twelve Steps and Twelve Traditions and Alcoholics Anonymous.* New York: AA World Services, 1981.

Prayer, Meditation, and Ritual

Achterberg, Jean, Barbara Dossey, and Leslie Kolkmeir. *Rituals for Healing: Using Imagery for Health and Wellness.* New York: Bantam Books, 1994.

Borysenko, Joan. *Pocketful of Miracles: Prayers, Meditations and Affirmations.* New York: Warner Books, 1994.

Dossey, Larry. *Healing Words: The Power of Prayer, the Practice of Medicine.* New York: HarperCollins, 1993.

Foster, Richard. *Prayer: Finding the Heart's True Home.* New York: HarperCollins, 1992.

Hanh, Thich Nhat. *Living Buddha, Living Christ.* New York: Putnam, 1995.

———. *The Miracle of Mindfulness.* Boston: Beacon Press, 1975.

———. *Peace Is Every Step: The Path of Mindfulness in Everyday Life.* New York: Bantam Books, 1992.

———. *Present Moment, Wonderful Moment.* Berkeley, Calif.: Parrallax Press, 1990.

———. *The Sun Is My Heart.* Berkeley, Calif.: Parrallax Press, 1988.

———. *Touching Peace.* Berkeley, Calif.: Parrallax Press, 1992.

Hays, Edward. *Prayers for a Planetary Pilgrim: A Personal Manual for Prayer and Ritual.* Leavenworth, Kans.: Forest of Peace Books, Inc., 1989.

Nepo, Mark. *The Book of Awakening: Having the Life You Want by Being Present to the Life You Have.* Berkeley, Calif.: Conari Press, 2000.

O'Donohue, John. *Anam Cara.* New York: HarperCollins, 1997.

———. *Echoes of Memory.* Cliffs of Moher, County Claire, Ireland: Salmon Publishing, Ltd., 1997.

———. *Eternal Echoes.* New York: HarperCollins, 1999.

Wellness and Holistic Self-Care

Benson, Herbert. *Beyond the Relaxation Response*. New York: Avon Books, 1976.

———. *The Relaxation Response*. New York: Avon Books, 1976.

Benson, Herbert, and Eileen Stuart. *The Wellness Book: The Comprehensive Guide to Maintaining Health and Treating Stress Related Illness*. New York: Fireside, 1992.

Cass, Hyla. *Kava, Nature's Answer to Stress, Anxiety, and Insomnia*. N.p.: Terrence McNally, 1998.

Davis, Martha. *The Relaxation and Stress Reduction Workbook*. Oakland, Calif.: New Harbinger Publications, Inc., 1988.

Gordon, James. *Manifesto for a New Medicine*. New York: Addison-Wesley, 1996.

Ivker, Robert S. *The Complete Self-Care Guide to Holistic Medicine*. New York: Tarcher, 2000.

McCallum, Pat. *Stepping Free of Limiting Patterns with Essence Repatterning*. Chevy Chase, Md.: Source Unlimited, 1992. (www.infinite.org/repatterning)

Novey, Donald W. *The Clinician's Complete Reference to Complementary and Alternative Medicine*. St. Louis, Miss.: Mosby, 2000.

Dreamwork

Percept Orientation and Language, developed by John Weir, Ph.D.,
San Luis Obispo, California

Donna Lee Graham, L.C.S.W.
R.D. 4 Box 292
Hedgesville, WV 25427

Donna is an extraordinary psychotherapist, teacher, and
trainer who has conducted dream groups and trainings nationwide
based on the Percept Orientation approach. Donna is an excellent
resource person for therapists, healers, and individuals interested
in exploring dreams.

Nicotine Addiction

CIG-NO Advantages
M.E. Cody Products, Inc.
41 Bergenline Ave.
Westwood, NJ 07675
1-800-431-2582

Natural herbal smoking deterrent products in flower essence
format and capsules designed to help break the nicotine habit.
Reduces nicotine cravings and withdrawal symptoms; safe and fast
acting. FDA and Health Canada registered. Recommended as a safe
tool for breaking free from nicotine addiction.

Spirituality: Ritual, Storytelling, Sacred Space, Community

Arrien, Angeles. *The Four-Fold Way: Walking the Paths of the Warrior, Teacher, Healer and Visionary.* New York: HarperCollins, 1993.

Barks, Coleman. *The Essential Rumi.* New York: HarperCollins, 1995.

Collins, Terah Kathryn. *The Western Guide to Feng Shui.* New York: HarperCollins, 1996.

Feldman, Christina, and Jack Kornfield. *Stories of the Spirit, Stories of the Heart: Parables of the Spiritual Path from Around the World.* New York: HarperCollins, 1991.

Fox, Matthew. *The Coming of the Cosmic Christ.* San Francisco: Harper & Row, 1988.

Hicks, Jerry, and Esther Hicks. *A New Beginning I.* San Antonio, Tex.: Abraham-Hicks Publications, 1988. (Box 690070, San Antonio, TX 78269; [830] 755-2299; www.abraham-hicks.com)

———. *A New Beginning II.* San Antonio, Tex.: Abraham-Hicks Publications, 1991. (Box 690070, San Antonio, TX 78269; [830] 755-2299; www.abraham-hicks.com)

Hillman, James. *The Soul's Code.* New York: Warner Books, 1996.

Linn, Denise. *Sacred Space: Altars.* New York: Ballantine Books, 1995.

Moore, Thomas. *Care of the Soul.* New York: HarperCollins, 1996.

———. *The Re-Enchantment of Everyday Life.* New York: HarperCollins, 1996.

———. *Soulmates.* New York: HarperCollins, 1994.

Ornish, Dean. *Love and Survival: The Scientific Basis for the Healing Power of Intimacy.* New York: HarperCollins, 1998.

Simpkinson, Charles, and Anne Simpkinson. *Sacred Stories: A Celebration of the Power of Stories to Transform and Heal.* San Francisco: HarperSanFrancisco, 1993.

Twyman, James. *Emissary of Light.* New York: Warner Books, 1998. (www.emissaryoflight.com)

Vanzant, Iyanla. *One Day My Soul Just Opened Up: 40 Days and 40 Nights Toward Spiritual Strength and Personal Growth.* New York: Fireside, 1998.

Williamson, Gay, and David Williamson. *Transformative Rituals: Celebrations for Personal Growth.* Deerfield Beach, Fla.: Health Communications Inc., 1994.

Bibliography

Achterberg, Jean, Barbara Dossey, and Leslie Kolkmeir. *Rituals for Healing: Using Imagery for Health and Wellness*. New York: Bantam Books, 1994.

Alcoholics Anonymous Comes of Age. New York: Harper & Row, 1967.

Alcoholics Anonymous World Services, Inc. *Alcoholics Anonymous*. New York: AA World Services, Inc., 1976.

———. *As Bill Sees It*. New York: AA World Services, Inc., 1967.

———. *Pass It On*. New York: AA World Services, Inc., 1984.

———. *Twelve Steps and Twelve Traditions*. New York: AA World Services, Inc., 1981.

Arrien, Angeles. *The Four-Fold Way: Walking the Paths of the Warrior, Teacher, Healer and Visionary*. New York: HarperCollins, 1993.

Barks, Coleman. *The Essential Rumi*. New York: HarperCollins, 1995.

Beck, Peggy V., and Anna L. Walters. *The Sacred Ways of Knowledge, Sources of Life*. Tsaile (Navajo Nation), Ariz.: Navajo Community College Press, 1988.

Benson, Herbert. *Timeless Healing: The Power of Biology and Belief*. New York: Scribner, 1996.

Benson, Herbert, and Eileen Stuart. *The Wellness Book: The Comprehensive Guide to Maintaining Health and Treating Stress Related Illness*. New York: Fireside, 1992.

Borysenko, Joan. *Pocketful of Miracles: Prayers, Meditations and Affirmations*. New York: Warner Books, 1994.

Cameron, Julia. *The Artist's Way: A Spiritual Path to Higher Creativity*. New York: Putnam, 1992.

Collins, Terah Katheryn. *The Western Guide to Feng Shui*. New York: HarperCollins, 1996.

cummings, e.e. *Complete Poems*. New York: Harcourt Brace Jovanovich,1923.

Dechter, Jacqueline. *Nicholas Roerich: The Life and Art of a Russian Master*. Rochester, Vt.: Park Street Press, 1989.

Feldman, Christina, and Jack Kornfield. *Stories of the Spirit, Stories of the Heart: Parables of the Spiritual Path from Around the World*. New York: HarperCollins, 1991.

Grof, Christina. *The Thirst for Wholeness: Attachment, Addiction, and the Spiritual Path*. New York: HarperCollins, 1993.

Hanh, Thich Nhat. *Present Moment, Wonderful Moment*. Berkeley, Calif.: Parallax Press, 1991.

Hicks, Jerry, and Esther Hicks. *A New Beginning (I and II)*. San Antonio, Tex.: Abraham-Hicks Publications, 1988, 1991.

Ivker, Robert S. *The Complete Self-Care Guide to Holistic Medicine*. New York: Tarcher, 2000.

Jung, C. G. "Letter to Bill Wilson." In *Pass It On: The Story of Bill Wilson and How the AA Message Reached the World,* pp. 382–85. New York: Alcoholics Anonymous World Services, Inc., 1984.

Kelly, Marcia, and Jack Kelly. *The Whole Heaven Catalogue.* Bell Tower, 1998.

Lifton, Robert J. *Death In Life: Survivors of Hiroshima.* New York: Basic Books, 1967.

May, Gerald. *Addiction and Grace.* New York: Harper, 1988.

Moore, Thomas. *The Re-Enchantment of Everyday Life.* New York: HarperCollins, 1996.

O'Donohue, John. *Eternal Echoes.* New York: HarperCollins, 1999.

Ornish, Dean. *Love and Survival.* New York: HarperCollins, 1998.

Small, Jacquelyn. *Awakening in Time: The Journey from Codependence to Co-Creation.* New York: Bantam Books, 1991.

Sparks, Tav. *The Wide Open Door: The Twelve Steps, Spiritual Tradition and the New Psychology.* Center City, Minn.: Hazelton Educational Materials, 1993.

Twenty-Four Hours a Day. Center City, Minn.: Hazelton Foundation, 1975.

Webb, Terry. *The Tree of Renewed Life.* New York: The Crossroad Publishing Company, 1992.

Whitfield, Charles. *Spirituality in Recovery.* Rutherford, N.J.: Perrin and Tregget, 1985.

Whyte, David. *The Heart Aroused.* New York: Doubleday, 1994.

Wright, Machaelle Small. *Flower Essences: Re-Ordering Our Understanding and Approach to Illness and Health.* Jeffersonton, Va.: Perelandra Ltd., 1988.

Index

AA. *See* Alcoholics Anonymous
acceptance, 44
addiction, classification of,
    15–16
addiction and recovery,
    personal stories of, 7–19
    See also recovery process
alcohol addiction
    Roger's story of, 13–19
    spirituality and, 25–26
Alcoholics Anonymous (AA)
    addiction described in,
    16–17
    community healing of,
    31–32
    as spiritual fellowship,
    26–27
    use of prayer, perspective
    on, 64

alienation and isolation, 40,
    44–45
altars, sacred, 145–46
amazing grace. *See* grace
anxiety, 130
autoimmune diseases, 157

Bach Flower Remedies, 11, 197
Beannacht (O'Donohue), 87–88
beauty and sacred order
    creating, 137–41
    healing power of, 135–37
    impact of, 141–46
behaviors
    compulsive, 115
    habitual, 148
    self-destructive, 92
beliefs, 150
belonging, sense of, 44–45

Benediction (O'Donohue),
   87–88
body/mind/spirit, healthy,
   148–52
botanical medicine, 160–61
"Breaking Free," celebration of,
   205
breathing exercises, 81–84
Buddhist prayer, 71

caffeine consumption, 147
candle-lighting rituals, 70,
   120–21
change, planting seeds of,
   121–23
CHI-ROBICS, 152–53
clean living, 137
cognitive strategies, 48–51,
   151–52
Cohen, Michael, 45
community healing
   essence of, 29–33
   suggestions for creating,
      33–40
compulsive behaviors, 115
control strategies, 14
crisis, concept of, 7

daily tasks, 40–44
dedications, 125–27
dental care, 136
disorganization, strategy for,
   140
divorce, 25
dream groups, creating,
   176–78
dream journals, 175

dreams
   benefits of, 168–69
   dimensions of, 165–68
   honoring, action in, 176
   nature of, perspective on,
      169–70
   remembering, process of,
      174–75
   ritual for nourishing,
      129–30
   transformation power of,
      171–74
dreamwork
   Percept Orientation method,
      170–74
   remembering dreams,
      174–75
drug addiction, Roger's story
   of, 13–19

earth blessings prayer, 75–76
earth walk, 154–55
Eastern medicine, 152–53
eating habits, 147
emotions, 150
energy flow, 152–53
ETS (Emergency Trauma
   Solution), 199
exercise, lack of, 147
   See also focusing exercises

fear(s)
   Jane's story of, 93–95
   practice for releasing,
      123–24
   ritual for cleansing,
      128–29

feng shui, principles of,
137–39
fight or flight response, 79
flower essences, benefits of, 11,
197–201
focusing exercises
for building intimacy, 38–40
for embracing the new day,
153–54
for inner awareness, 52–54,
159–60
for stress reduction, 48–54,
80–84
using your imagination,
51–52, 154–55
freedom of choice, 95–96

grace
concept of, 183–84
experiences of, 184–88,
190–92
grace map journals, 188–90
gratitude prayer, 74
greeting the day, 119, 153–54
group meetings, 32
guided imagery, 157–59

habitual behaviors, 148
harmony and balance,
achieving, 125, 139
health and well-being
in everyday life, 135–37
promoting, 137–41
See also immune system
function
health practitioners, prayer for,
70–71

heartfelt prayer, 57
herbs, healing power of,
160–61
Hess, Elizabeth, 27
holistic medicine, 18, 30
hopelessness, sense of, 159
hygiene, poor personal, 136,
147

imagination, exercise in,
51–52, 154–55
Immune Herbal Formula, 161
immune system function
improving efficiency of,
147–51
interventions for
botanical medicines, 160–61
cognitive strategies, 151–52
focusing techniques, 159–60
gentle exercises, 152–55
mental imagery, 157–59
mission statement, 162–63
touch healing, 155–57
vitamin C, 161–62
inner peace, sense of, 72,
141–43
intimacy, exercise for building,
38–40
isolation, sense of, 40, 44–45

journaling
grace map journal, 188–90
healing benefits of, 180–82
writing process, 182–83

limitation and possibility,
Gary's story of, 90–92

living environment
   feng shui principles, 137–41
   influence on well-being,
      135–37
   See also beauty and sacred
      order
living space, restructuring, 139
Lovingkindness prayer, 71

mantra, 83
McNeill, John, 30
mealtime prayer, 72–73
meditations for healing
   benefits of, 58–61, 76–80
   definition of, 56
   eating meditation, 86–87
   relaxation practices,
      examples of, 81–85
   walking meditation, 85–86
men's support groups, 34–35
mental imagery, 157–59
mind-body medicine, 148–52
mindfulness practices. *See*
   meditations
mission statements, 162–63
morning prayer, 70–71

Narcotics Anonymous (NA), 31
Natural Herbal Essences, 161
natural medicine, 11, 197–201
nature, connecting with, 44–45
   See also living environment
neglect, personal, 147
Nepo, Mark, 62
nicotine addiction, Barry's
   story of, 8–13

nightmares, 166

O'Donohue, John, 87
order and balance, creating,
   125, 139
outer-driven focus, 141

passion for living, 162–63
Percept Orientation method,
   170–74
Perelandra Flower Essences,
   198, 199
personalized prayer, 74
personal support teams,
   36–38
Placement Technique, 42–44
prayer and meditation
   effectiveness of, 58–61, 74
   healing power of, 55–59
prayer for healing
   benefits of, perspectives on,
      62–65
   Buddhist prayer, 71
   definition of, 56
   earth blessings prayer, 75–76
   gratitude prayer, 74
   for the health practitioner,
      70–71
   mealtime prayer, 72–73
   protection prayer, 72
   Serenity Prayer, 65–67
   St. Francis Prayer, 67–69
protection prayer, 72

Re-Connecting with Nature
   (Cohen), 45

recovery process
  community healing in, 29–40
  healing rituals in, 115–18
  honoring everyday life in, 135–37
  prayer and meditation in, 55–59, 76–80
  spirituality in, 21–27
  taking effective action in, 47–48
  See also dreams; self-reflection; storytelling
relapse, risk of, 145
relapse dreams, 166
relationship addiction, 24–25
relationships
  exercise for building, 38–40
  ritual for ending, 127–28
relaxation practices, 81–85
relaxation response, 78–79
responsibility, personal, 151
retreats, benefits from, 194–96
retreats, healing benefits from, 194–95
rituals, healing
  nature and value of, 115–18
  selection of
    breaking free of destructive patterns, 131–33
    candle-lighting, 70, 120–21
    cleansing fears and doubts, 128–29
    cleansing self-limiting thoughts, 130–31

    creating order and balance, 125
    ending a relationship, 127–28
    greeting the day, 119
    making a dedication, 125–27
    nourishing your dreams, 129–30
    planting seeds of change, 121–23
    practice for releasing fears, 123–24

same-gender support groups, 34–36
sanctuaries, 139, 192
self-absorption, 56–57
selflessness, 68
self-reflection, tools for
  grace map journal, 188–90
  journaling, 180–83
Seneca House, 18
Serenity Prayer, 65–67
Shaker song, 141
sleep deprivation, 147
smoking. *See* nicotine addiction
sobriety, 19
Sources of Life: Sacred Ways of Knowledge, The (Beck and Walters), 99
spiritual awakenings, 25–26, 58
spiritual directors, 34
spirituality, definition of, 21–27

sponsorship, 32, 33–34
St. Francis Prayer, 67–69
stimulants, use of, 147
stinking thinking, 159
story circle, creating a, 112–14,
    189
storytelling, healing art of
    creating a community circle,
        112–14, 189
    stories of
        drug addiction, 13–19
        essence of life, 206–207
        facing our fears, 93–95
        faith and love, 106–7
        freedom of expression,
            107–8
        gathering of angels,
            104–5
        limitation and possibility,
            90–92
        love and support, 109–12
        nicotine addiction, 8–13
        power of choice, 95–96
        stages of addiction, 100–4
    summary of characteristics,
        108–9
    teaching a story, 96–97
    as transformation tool, 7–8,
        89–90, 92, 98–100
stressors, 147, 157
stress reduction, tools for
    focusing exercises for,
        48–54, 80–81
    meditation for, 77

support groups, 33

Taking a Chance on God
    (McNeill), 30
therapy groups, 38
thoughts
    impact on well-being, 150
    limiting patterns of, 92
    ritual for cleaning self-
        limiting, 130–31
to-do lists, designing,
    40–44
touch, healing power of,
    155–57
toxicity, 166
transformation prayer,
    62–63
tribal healing, 30

vitamin C supplements,
    161–62
voice recorders, 175
volunteers, 34

walk, taking an earth,
    154–55
walking meditation, 85–86
Waterfall of Hands, A (Nepo),
    62
withdrawal symptoms, 60
women's support groups,
    34–35
working environment. *See*
    living environment

About the Authors

B arry A. Sultanoff, M.D., is a graduate of Cornell University and the University of Rochester School of Medicine. His home-based practice in Kensington, Maryland emphasizes the integration of body, mind, and spirit, blending psychotherapy, whole-person medicine, and holistic health education. He incorporates principles of feng shui into his practice and is a charter member of the Feng Shui Guild.

Dr. Sultanoff is a founding member and former board member of the American Holistic Medical Association. He has written for *Natural Health Magazine, Townsend Letter for Doctors,* and the *Journal of the American Holistic Medical Association.* An internationally known speaker, he has presented at the First International Conference on Holistic Medicine, the First Congress on High-Tech Medicine, the United Nations Habitat II Conference, and the Creative Health Network, among others, and makes daily televised health announcements in Fairfax, Virginia. He has recently produced, in collaboration with musician Paul Reisler, a compact disk entitled *Breathe! Creating an Inner Environment of Peace.*

Dr. Sultanoff is also an avid Argentine tango dancer, amateur photographer, yogi, in-line skater, and poet; he recently appeared at the U.S. Library of Congress as part of poet laureate Robert Pinsky's "Favorite Poems" project.

Roger F. Klinger, M.T.S, is a graduate of Harvard Divinity School, with doctoral training at Howard University Divinity School and postgraduate training at the Rutgers School of Alcohol and Drug Studies. He currently serves as Director of Counseling Ministry, an innovative holistic counseling and education center with offices in Washington D.C. and Rappahanock County, Virginia. He is an adjunct professor of Pastoral Care and Counseling at Virginia Theological Seminary and Wesley Seminary in Washington D.C.

His areas of expertise include addictions, stress management, the psychology of healing, and the relationship between spiritual development, growth, community, creativity and optimal health. Roger is a freelance writer and inspirational speaker, and maintains a national phone-consulting practice that includes counseling, spiritual direction, and business coaching/training for individuals and organizations, helping executives, business leaders, and health-care practitioners to integrate spirituality into their work.

Roger is also an artist, poet, world traveler, naturalist, and avid gardener; he spends half his time at Dancing Tree, a contemplative sanctuary and retreat center that he built and founded on ten acres of beautiful mountain land in the Virginia countryside.

For additional information, contact:

Counseling Ministry

114 Mossie Lane

Amissville, Virginia 20106

dancingtree@erols.co